Business Travel

Business Travel

Rob Davidson

PITMAN
PUBLISHING

PITMAN PUBLISHING
128 Long Acre, London WC2E 9AN

A Division of Longman Group UK Limited

© Rob Davidson, 1994

First published in Great Britain 1994

British Library Cataloguing in Publication Data
A CIP catalogue record for this book can be obtained from the British Library.

ISBN 0 273 60415 5

Typeset by ROM-Data Corporation Ltd, Falmouth, Cornwall
Printed and bound in Great Britain by Clays Ltd, St Ives plc

The Publishers' policy is to use paper manufactured from sustainable forests.

Contents

Preface

....

In recent years, business travel has emerged as one of the fastest-growing and most profitable sectors of the travel and tourism industry. Travel for business-related purposes, in the widest sense – including meetings and conferences, trade fairs and exhibitions, as well as incentive travel – has been widely recognised as one of the most effective ways of doing business, seeking out new markets, exchanging ideas, and communicating with colleagues and customers alike.

The combination of recession, political upheaval and regional conflicts which have characterised this decade has done little to diminish the ever-increasing volume of business travel worldwide.

Nevertheless, the 1990s have seen a number of significant changes, which are having far-reaching implications for all buyers and suppliers of business travel: important shifts in consumption patterns, great advances in transport and communications technology, and changes in the world's political and economic composition. All of these developments are having a major impact on business travel and will provide the principal challenges to the business travel sector for the years immediately ahead.

The rise of the importance of the tourism industry in general and its recognition as a major economic force have been paralleled by growth in the provision of further and higher education travel and tourism courses in Britain and overseas. During the last ten years, there have been great advances in the quality and quantity of travel and tourism education at all levels. At the same time, the importance of continuing education and training for those already employed in travel and tourism has been widely recognised as a vital ingredient in the process of keeping up-to-date with changing circumstances and new techniques.

As those teaching travel and tourism have increasingly come to perceive business travel as a vitally-important sector of the industry, it has finally begun to have the prominence it merits in educational syllabuses – as an option or specialisation, or as an entire course. Examples of this range from the ABTA National Training Board/City & Guilds NVQ Certificate in Business Travel award, through the BTEC National Award in Travel and Tourism's option in Conference and Exhibition Organisation, to the various degree-level courses with Business Travel options.

Business Travel is the first textbook to cover the full range of business travel activity in detail. While textbooks and case studies based on holiday and leisure travel abound, until now no substantial work on business travel has been written.

This textbook provides a comprehensive, chapter-by-chapter analysis of the business travel industry in its widest sense. After an introductory scene-setting chapter, there follow three chapters dealing with the principal forms of business travel: conferences, incentive travel, and exhibitions and trade shows. The next three chapters examine the role of the transport, accommodation, and retail travel sectors in providing for the needs of business travellers. In each case, there is an analysis of current and future trends in the sector, drawing on official statistics and articles from the press, as well as published reports.

The emphasis in *Business Travel* is on practical information, selected to make the reader aware of the main issues and developments in this field. To this end, the book contains a number of detailed, contemporary case studies drawn from business travel organisations and companies in Britain and overseas.

Another important feature of the book are the student activities which appear at the end of each chapter. In order to test the reader's understanding, each chapter finishes with questions on the text, practical assignments and a checklist of key terms found in the chapter.

The textbook will appeal to two different types of reader:

1 Students of travel and tourism in further and higher education. The language and content of the book are pitched at a such a level as to be accessible not only to City & Guilds and BTEC-level students but also to those undertaking degree-level work at universities.

2 Practitioners already employed in business travel. Those working in one of the sectors of this industry will benefit from a text which not only gives them up-to-date and practical information which is

highly relevant to their sector but also provides them with an overview of the entire industry. In this way, *Business Travel* will form a key element of their in-service training programmes.

Business Travel will enable both types of reader to add considerably to their understanding of this exhilarating and dynamic sector of the travel and tourism industry, which has remained for too long eclipsed by the sun, sea, and sand image usually evoked by any mention of that industry.

R. Davidson

November 1993

1

Tourism for business

WHAT IS BUSINESS TOURISM?

Business tourism is concerned with people travelling for purposes which are related to their work. As such, it represents one of the oldest forms of tourism, man having travelled for the purposes of trade since very early times.

Travel for business purposes may be contrasted with other forms of tourist activity such as holidays, short breaks or visits to friends and relatives. Business tourism is very often overshadowed in importance by the sun-and-fun image of holiday travel. And yet, not only does business tourism have a glamour, dynamism and exoticism all of its own, it also occupies a huge sector of the tourism market, which is immensely important to destinations where it takes place. In 1990 alone, out of a total of 425 million international trips made throughout the world, *63 million* were made for business purposes.

Travel for work-related purposes can take several forms. The main categories are: general business travel, meetings, exhibitions, and incentive travel.

General business travel

General business travel involves people working away from their normal place of employment for a short period of time. A manager who suddenly has to fly from London to his company's Brussels office in order to sort out some problem would be an example of this. Some people have jobs which mean that they are often 'on the road', travelling to other cities or countries for short periods. For sales representatives or journalists, for example, business travel can be an integral part of the job.

Meetings

A very common reason for travelling away from home is to attend a meeting. This can be one person travelling by train to discuss business with a few colleagues in a nearby city; or it can be many hundreds of delegates descending on one city from all over the world to spend a week attending an annual sales conference. Product launches are another kind of meeting, when company employees, the press, and other interested parties are invited to the unveiling of a new model of car or a new range of cosmetics, for example.

Trade fairs and exhibitions

Trade fairs and trade exhibitions are vast events which attract two types of business visitor to the cities in which they are held: the exhibitors themselves, who attend in order to promote their service or product, and the actual visitors who come with a professional interest. For example, 'Hotelympia' is an annual trade fair held at the Olympia Exhibition Centre in London. The exhibitors are the representatives of the companies who manufacture equipment or provide services for the hotel industry, and the visitors are the many thousands of hotel owners and managers from the UK and overseas who come to examine, and perhaps buy, what is being promoted.

Incentive travel

Companies which wish to reward their highest-achieving employees, or encourage them to perform better, can do so by sending them on all-expenses-paid incentive trips, for a short period. This usually takes the form of a very luxurious short holiday for such employees (and very often their spouses), with the emphasis on entertainment, relaxation and pleasure. Although no actual work is done on behalf of the company, the reason for travelling is very closely connected with the participant's working life, and as such, makes incentive travel a form of business tourism.

It is, however, a characteristic of the business tourism market that the different categories often merge into one another and cannot always be clearly categorised into one of the above forms. Many conferences, for example, are accompanied by an exhibition on the same theme.

Organisers of a conference on some aspect of a specialised medical field, for example, may well invite representatives of pharmaceutical companies to buy exhibition space in a hall close to where the conference is to be held. Not only does this offset the cost of the conference from the organiser's point of view, but it also gives the pharmaceutical companies the opportunity to exhibit their products to the right market – and gives the delegates another reason for attending.

Similarly, when a conference is held in an exotic destination such as Singapore or the Bahamas, an employer, in selecting a member of staff to attend, may really be awarding him or her some kind of incentive reward for work well done.

BUSINESS TOURISM AND LEISURE TOURISM

Most sectors of the tourism industry serve both the business and the leisure market. Accommodation, transport, the retail travel trade, tourism promotion and information services, and even tourist attractions will normally cater for both markets – although the services they provide to each may be different.

Nevertheless, there are some important distinctions between these two types of tourism. These are shown in Figure 1.1.

Distinguishing business travellers from those travelling for leisure purposes is far from easy. In reality, it is never as clean-cut a distinction as simply 'pin-stripes or bermudas?'. Jeans and tee-shirts are to be found in business class compartments and groups of besuited conference delegates may be seen strolling around Disneyland.

The two categories of tourism are very far from being distinct and watertight. Business tourism, in particular, can involve a substantial leisure element. Incentive travel, for example, may consist entirely of leisure, sport or entertainment. But, even for conference delegates, visitors to trade fairs and individual business travellers, excursions to local restaurants and places of entertainment, or sightseeing tours, can be a way of relaxing at the end of the working day. Socialising in this way can be an important part of the business tourism experience for groups, as it gives delegates or colleagues the opportunity to unwind together and get to know each other on a less formal basis.

	Leisure tourism	Business tourism	but . . . .
Who pays?	The tourist	The traveller's employer or association	Self-employed business travellers are paying for their own trips
Who decides on the destination?	The tourist	The organiser of the meeting/ incentive trip/conference/ exhibition	Organisers will often take into account delegates' wishes
When do trips take place?	During classic holiday periods and at weekends	All year round, Monday to Friday	July and August are avoided for major events
Lead time? (period of time between booking and going on the trip)	Holidays usually booked a few months in advance; short breaks, a few days	Some business trips must be made at very short notice	Major conferences are booked many years in in advance
Who travels?	Anyone with the necessary spare time and money	Those whose work requires them to travel, or members of associations	Not all business trips involve managers on white-collar duties
What kinds of destination are used?	All kinds: coastal, city, mountain, and countryside locations	Largely centred on cities in industrialised countries	Incentive destinations are much the same as for up-market holidays

Figure 1.1   Leisure tourism and business tourism

The distinction between the two categories of tourism is further blurred by the presence of 'accompanying persons' alongside many business tourism events. Incentive travel often includes the husbands or wives of those selected for such trips. But also, it is not uncommon for those travelling to exotic destinations for conferences or trade fairs and exhibitions to take their spouses along and make a short holiday out of the trip. In such cases, the couple may prolong their stay in order to have the time to tour around the destination after the business part of the trip is over.

ADVANTAGES OF BUSINESS TOURISM FOR THE DESTINATION

Business tourism offers many advantages to the destinations where it takes place. Many of these advantages are the same as those created by leisure tourism: the need to maintain an attractive environment, good transport links and commercial infrastructure, for example. But business tourism brings several of its own advantages to local residents and businesspeople.

Greater profitability

Generally speaking, business tourism is relatively high-cost and therefore high-yielding. Because of the socio-economic profile of those travelling on business – often the upper and middle management classes – business tourism tends to bring benefits to those suppliers catering for the upper end of the market: three-stars plus hotels, first-class transport facilities, and so on.

The benefits of business tourism spending are also spread throughout the community, and are not restricted to hotels or conference centres and airlines or train services. When conferences, trade fairs and business meetings, for example, are accompanied by social and leisure events, this brings benefits to restaurants, tourist and cultural attractions, local transport services, guides and shops at the destination.

Seasonal spread

An immense advantage of business tourism to destinations is its timing – *when* conference delegates, trade fair visitors and so on arrive in town

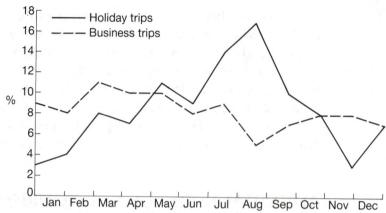

Figure 1.2   The United Kingdom Tourist Survey
Source: The British Tourist Authority

is an important consideration. Because so much business tourism takes place in the off-peak season for holidays, many destinations rely on business visitors to offset the effects of seasonality. So when the summer is over and the holidaymakers have left Blackpool, for example, the town's hoteliers, restaurateurs and taxi drivers can turn to the delegates attending the annual political party conferences, for a few more weeks of profitable business.

The complementarity in seasonal spread for holidays and for business trips in the UK is shown in Figure 1.2.

Environmental impact

Business tourists are among the most environmentally-friendly visitors imaginable. Their nuisance-effect on the local population is minimal. Although conference delegates, for example, often descend in droves on the destination, they spend most of their days indoors, deep in discussion and out of sight. They are not taking up valuable space on the beach, in the bus or in the Post Office queue. It is true that in the evening they may stroll around a little in their suits and name-badges, but only the most nervous of local residents will be worried by this.

Certain types of business tourist also offer the advantage of favouring public transport, arriving most often by train or by plane. This means that they neither add to traffic congestion at the destination nor enrage local people by taking up 'their' parking spaces – that infamous visitor-versus-resident bone of contention.

Promotional possibilities

A business visitor who leaves with a good impression of the conference, trade fair or incentive destination becomes an unpaid ambassador for that place. This explains why local authorities make such an effort to impress business visitors to their town or region. These are often influential people, whose opinions of the destination will be instrumental in determining its image in the minds of others who have not visited it.

Local efforts to impress can take several forms: a speech from the mayor to open a conference, a film of local attractions, a civil banquet attended by local dignitaries, or a coach tour of the town and its surroundings, laid on by the local council. Whatever the technique, the aim is always to create a good image, not only so that business tourists will spread the word among family, friends and colleagues, but also in the hope that they may either return on holiday or even decide to relocate or set up a branch of their business in the locality.

PROMOTING BUSINESS TOURISM

Because of the many advantages to destinations of having high-spending, low-impact visitors in their city or country, competition for the business tourist is intense.

But how much choice do business tourists have, as to where they go on their trips? For many, namely those on general business travel trips, the answer is very little. If the problem to be sorted out is in the company's Glasgow branch, then that determines the destination, whether the fix-it manager would rather travel to Paris, or not. In other words, general business travel is *non-discretionary*.

On the other hand, conferences, exhibitions, and incentive travel are entirely discretionary: those in charge of organising them *can*, if the conditions are right, be persuaded to hold them in Birmingham instead of Edinburgh, or in Rio de Janeiro instead of Hong Kong.

National tourism organisations and individual cities' tourism offices are the principal promotional bodies responsible for attracting business tourism to their destinations. Most such organisations have a department whose sole function it is to promote the destination to the business tourism market. At the level of individual cities in the UK, for example, tourist boards are increasingly calling themselves 'Visitor and Convention Bureaux', emphasising the business as well as the leisure tourism aspects of their role.

Incoming business tourists have the added advantage of bringing valuable foreign currency into the country, and this explains why the British Tourist Authority (BTA) places such emphasis on inbound business tourism to the UK. The figures speak for themselves: one in four of all visitors to the UK comes on business. Business visitors spend about £1.5 billion in the UK every year, averaging more than £500 on each trip. Business visitors spend more than twice as much as the average daily expenditure for all types of visitor.

What are the UK's assets as an international business destination? The BTA states them as follows:

● It has the best international air connections in the world. Heathrow and Gatwick are major hub-and-spoke airports, and London is the European gateway for non-stop flights from Tokyo and Hong Kong. There are other growing entry points such as Birmingham and Manchester.

● It is a compact country with excellent internal communications, and world-famous places suitable for incentives and post-conference, add-on trips.

● The English language is the language of international business and is also the language in which most international conferences are run.

HOW THE BTA PROMOTES THE UK AS A BUSINESS DESTINATION

Most of the efforts to attract conferences, incentive trips and trade fair visitors to Britain is coordinated from the London headquarters of the BTA, through their Business Travel department. The Business Travel team works in close cooperation with business tourism suppliers in the UK and with a number of Business Travel Managers who are based in the BTA's overseas offices.

Business tourism suppliers are those businesses providing facilities or services for the various sectors of the business tourism market. They can be, for example, exhibition and conference centres, hotels which target the business market, or transport operators such as British Airways or British Rail, which benefit considerably from business traffic. Another important supplier is the destination management company. They provide a specialised service to those companies or organisations in need of someone to organise a conference, incentive trip or product launch, for example, on their behalf. Not only can they come up with interesting ideas for such events, they can also undertake all the detailed organising.

Here are the main ways in which the BTA works in this sector:

Joint schemes

Each year, the BTA enters into joint scheme arrangements with over 50 major venues, industry organisations, exhibition organisers, conference organisers and convention bureaux, to promote British business travel facilities and events to the overseas markets. The financial assistance available from the BTA can take the form of helping to meet the costs of brochure production, direct mail, or overseas advertising and overseas promotional events.

The amount of BTA subvention is negotiable, but is usually limited to about 20 per cent of the total promotion cost. The BTA also gives free advice on the planning of overseas promotion for business travel services.

Promotional print

The BTA edits and prints a range of specialised guides and booklets aimed at the overseas business market. Suppliers have the opportunity of buying advertising space in these publications, which are printed in various foreign languages and are distributed through the BTA's overseas offices.

Promotional events in Britain

Each year, the BTA organises a number of business travel exhibitions and workshops in the UK, inviting potential buyers from overseas to attend, in order to meet suppliers and discuss, for example, their conference or incentive travel needs together.

Familiarisation trips to Britain

Potential buyers, such as conference or incentive travel organisers based overseas, as well as representatives of the foreign business travel press, are also invited by the BTA to participate in an annual series of familiarisation trips. These take them to different locations in the UK, where they can see for themselves the facilities such as conference centres, exhibition halls and hotels aiming at the incentive market.

Overseas missions

Every year, the BTA organises a series of overseas mini-workshops called missions, which are suitable for conference and incentive suppliers, as well as those offering services to the individual business traveller. These allow British participants to bring their products to the market-place and discuss business on a one-to-one basis with potential buyers.

In Europe, these usually take place in the autumn months, when potential buyers are planning their programmes for the following year. The format of these missions varies from country to country, according to the national customs. For example, the BTA Paris office organises *déjeuners d'affaires*, which enable British representatives to meet and present their facilities to select small groups of contacts. Other formats include breakfast seminars, morning sessions followed by a luncheon, cocktail presentations and/or full-day sessions, with promotional dinners.

The overseas staff of the BTA take great care to identify suitable potential buyers, matching them to the range of business travel products represented by the British participants in these missions. In this way, the 'right' people meet each other to discuss business.

Direct mail services

As part of its range of promotional opportunities offered to British suppliers, the BTA has developed business travel databases of contacts in key markets. These have been compiled through personal contact, telemarketing and direct mail research.

These mailing lists enable suppliers to target direct mail campaigns to specific contact groups. The broad categories include the following:

> Corporate contacts
> Associations
> Meeting planners
> Incentive travel specialists
> Travel agencies with specialist business travel interests (including
>   implants in large corporate premises)
> Business travel press

Suppliers can choose any combination of the above categories, or one country or region of a country. The BTA provides a complete mailing service, offering the whole service, and not the actual lists. Material for mailing is supplied to a mailing house.

....

**CASE
STUDY**

EIBTM 93

There are a number of overseas exhibitions targeted at buyers in the incentive travel, conference, and business travel markets. These are large trade fairs, where the exhibitors are the representatives of business tourism destinations and suppliers to the business tourism industry; and the visitors are those responsible for buying in this market.

The two most important overseas exhibitions in the business tourism world are the European Incentives, Business Travel and Meetings show (EIBTM), held each year in Geneva, and the Incentive Travel and Meetings Exhibition (IT & ME), held in Chicago in the autumn of each year.

EIBTM is a truly international exhibition, to which buyers are flown by the organisers, EIBTM Ltd, from all over the world. Entry is on an invitation-only basis and, although attendance is very small compared with major trade shows such as the annual World Travel Market in London, the quality of the buyers is first rate. The EIBTM is probably the most expensive show of its type in the world, but it is usually worth every penny – for those who can afford it! The 1993 EIBTM exhibition was held on 11–13 May.

'Hosted buyer' is the name given by the organisers to the selected decision-makers who are flown to the show from all over the world, as guests of EIBTM Ltd. In 1993, the hosted buyers made up around 1,700 of the estimated 4,500 visitors who attended the show. All hosted buyers were given three scheduled group appointments during their visit.

The hosted buyer programme cost the organisers about £1.4 million, a great increase on previous years, due to a rapid expansion in the programme (in 1992, the show hosted 1,350 buyers). However, this represents money well spent, since the quality of the hosted buyers is very high.

In 1993, the total EIBTM display area topped 9,000 square metres compared with 7,000 the previous year. Over 80 countries were represented by 1,450 exhibitors in the two halls at Geneva's Palexpo Centre.

Most of this growth was due to exhibitors increasing the size of their stands (for example, the corporate hotel chains, Marriott and Hilton International), but there was also growth from new destinations exhibiting for the first time, such as the Ukraine, and the Baltic States of Lithuania and Estonia. In 1993, it was also noticeable that a higher proportion of the exhibition was devoted to developing countries within Latin America, Africa, and the Middle East.

For buyers visiting EIBTM for the first time, in addition to the international destinations on show, an educational conference programme ran alongside the show.

For the third year, the EIBTM campaign for the *Greening of Business Tourism* was publicised at the show. To bolster the campaign, there was the launch of a 'Green Clinic', to address environmental issues for meetings planners. Also available at the event was a new environmental handbook called *How to Plan Meetings that Don't Cost the Earth*, which aims to help conference and incentive buyers to integrate eco-tourism and conservation considerations into their work.

The EIBTM exhibition plans to increase investment in the hosted buyer programme to US$2.3 million (£1.58 million) in 1994.

BUSINESS TOURISM IN THE UK

What is the profile of business tourism in the UK? One of the most comprehensive accounts of this comes in the form of the annual *United Kingdom Tourism Survey*. Figure 1.3 gives the details of this sector for 1991, in terms of trips, nights and spending.

The tables also give global figures for trips, nights, and spending in 1989, 1990 as well as 1991. These show very clearly a sharp decline on all three counts during that period. A review of the recent history of business tourism reveals the reasons behind this trend.

	TRIPS					NIGHTS					SPENDING				
	United Kingdom	England	Scotland	Wales	Northern Ireland	United Kingdom	England	Scotland	Wales	Northern Ireland	United Kingdom	England	Scotland	Wales	Northern Ireland
	MILLIONS					MILLIONS					£ MILLIONS				
BUSINESS AND WORK TOURISM 1989	14.4	11.8	1.6	0.8	0.2	38.1	30.7	4.1	2.3	0.3	2,050	1,555	290	145	35
BUSINESS AND WORK TOURISM 1990	11.5	9.9	0.9	0.5	0.1	30.3	25.4	3.3	1.4	0.1	1,615	1,360	180	60	10
BUSINESS AND WORK TOURISM 1991	10.2	8.7	1.0	0.4	0.1	26.7	21.5	3.1	1.2	0.3	1,440	1,190	160	55	20
	%	%	%	%	%	%	%	%	%	%	%	%	%	%	%
ACCOMMODATION USED															
Hotel/motel/guesthouse	65	65	68	63	63	51	51	55	50	57	74	72	85	74	83
Paying guest in:															
– farmhouse	1	*	1	–	–	1	1	1	–	–	1	1	1	–	–
– other private house/bed & breakfast	4	4	5	10	–	5	5	4	11	–	3	3	4	4	–
Self-catering in rented:															
– flat/apartment	1	1	–	1	–	3	2	–	3	–	1	1	–	2	–
– house/chalet/villa/bungalow	1	1	1	–	–	1	2	3	–	–	*	*	*	–	–
– hostel/university/school	6	6	10	5	19	10	10	13	5	21	4	5	3	2	1
Friends'/relatives' home	12	13	9	6	18	12	13	7	4	20	9	10	2	3	15

Figure 1.3   Profile of business and work-related tourism in the UK

Source: The British Tourist Authority

BUSINESS AND WORK TOURISM IN THE UNITED KINGDOM

	TRIPS (MILLIONS)					NIGHTS (MILLIONS)					SPENDING (£ MILLIONS)				
	United Kingdom	England	Scotland	Wales	Northern Ireland	United Kingdom	England	Scotland	Wales	Northern Ireland	United Kingdom	England	Scotland	Wales	Northern Ireland
Own second home/timeshare	2	2	*	–	–	2	2	*	–	–	1	1	*	–	–
Holiday camp/village:															
– self-catering	*	*	–	–	–	1	1	–	–	–	*	*	–	–	–
– serviced	*	*	–	–	–	*	*	–	–	–	*	*	–	–	–
Camping	1	1	1	6	–	2	2	1	6	–	*	1	*	1	–
Caravan:															
– towed	1	1	–	6	–	2	2	–	12	–	1	1	–	11	–
– static, owned	*	*	*	–	–	*	*	1	–	–	*	*	*	–	–
– static, not owned	1	1	3	–	–	4	4	6	–	–	1	1	1	–	–
Boat	*	*	1	–	–	1	1	5	–	–	*	*	*	–	–
Sleeper cab of lorry/truck	1	1	*	1	–	1	1	*	1	–	*	*	–	1	–
Other/transit	4	4	3	4	5	4	4	4	8	2	4	4	2	3	1
Total commercial accommodation	75	74	79	84	63	69	68	69	83	57	82	80	92	92	83
Total non-commercial accommodation	26	27	24	16	43	31	32	31	17	43	18	20	8	8	17
Total serviced	69	69	74	73	63	57	57	60	61	57	78	76	91	78	83
Total self-catering	5	5	5	13	–	12	11	9	22	–	4	4	2	14	–

Figure 1.3 Continued

BUSINESS AND WORK TOURISM IN THE UNITED KINGDOM	TRIPS MILLIONS					NIGHTS MILLIONS					SPENDING £ MILLIONS				
	United Kingdom	England	Scotland	Wales	Northern Ireland	United Kingdom	England	Scotland	Wales	Northern Ireland	United Kingdom	England	Scotland	Wales	Northern Ireland
MAIN MODE OF TRANSPORT USED															
Train	11	11	10	5	–	11	10	12	6	–	13	15	5	4	–
Regular coach/bus	3	3	4	3	–	4	4	7	8	–	2	3	2	1	–
Organised coach tour	3	3	1	4	15	4	4	1	4	18	2	2	1	1	1
Car (owned)	66	69	50	69	15	64	69	46	68	11	59	64	34	70	10
Car (hired)	3	3	3	6	–	3	3	5	5	–	4	4	6	17	–
Campervan	*	*	–	1	–	*	*	–	2	–	*	*	–	*	–
Motorcycle	*	*	–	–	–	*	*	–	–	–	*	*	–	–	–
Bicycle	–	–	–	–	–	–	–	–	–	–	–	–	–	–	–
Plane	7	5	27	–	70	7	4	22	–	72	16	10	49	–	89
Boat/ship	1	*	2	*	–	2	*	5	*	–	*	*	*	1	–
Lorry/truck/van	5	5	3	10	–	5	5	2	7	–	3	3	3	5	–
Other mode of transport	*	*	*	1	–	*	*	*	*	–	*	*	*	1	–
Total personal transport	69	72	52	75	15	68	72	51	75	11	64	68	40	88	10
Total public transport	25	22	42	13	85	26	22	42	17	89	33	29	57	6	90
ORGANISATION OF TRIP															
Any booking through:															
– travel agent	8	7	16	2	42	9	8	14	1	51	15	13	29	3	58
– other commercial organisation	2	2	3	2	4	1	1	2	2	1	3	3	4	2	4
– non profit making organisation	3	3	3	5	14	4	4	2	5	9	2	2	2	3	5

Figure 1.3 Continued

BUSINESS AND WORK TOURISM IN THE UNITED KINGDOM	TRIPS MILLIONS					NIGHTS MILLIONS					SPENDING £ MILLIONS				
	United Kingdom	England	Scotland	Wales	Northern Ireland	United Kingdom	England	Scotland	Wales	Northern Ireland	United Kingdom	England	Scotland	Wales	Northern Ireland
Inclusive trip:	2	1	6	2	–	3	2	5	3	–	3	2	10	*	–
– inclusive trip via travel agent	1	*	4	–	–	2	1	3	–	–	2	1	9	–	–
– inclusive but not via travel agent	1	1	2	2	–	1	1	2	3	–	1	1	2	*	–
Travel agent used only for other items	7	7	12	2	42	8	7	11	1	51	13	12	21	3	58
No such arrangement	87	88	79	91	40	86	87	83	92	39	80	83	65	92	33
DURATION OF TRIP															
TOTAL 1–3 nights	79	80	75	70	73	45	48	34	41	48	71	71	75	57	60
TOTAL 4+ nights	21	20	25	30	27	55	52	66	59	52	29	29	25	43	40
Average duration of trip (nights)	2.6	2.5	3.3	2.8	2.9										

Figure 1.3 Continued

TRENDS

During the 1980s, business tourism – in the widest sense, including travel for all business purposes, meetings and conferences, exhibitions, and incentive travel – emerged as one of the fastest-growing and most lucrative sectors of the travel and tourism industry. Travel for business-related purposes was recognised as being one of the most effective ways of doing business, seeking out new markets, exchanging ideas, and communicating with colleagues and customers alike. Accompanying this explosion of business travel activity were the fast-growing numbers of travel and tourism professionals, whose skills and knowledge helped construct, organise, promote and sell the travel products increasingly sought after by client companies.

But the 1990s have brought a number of challenges to those working in the business tourism sector. It is these challenges which have set the agenda for the years ahead.

Recession and recovery

The early 1990s were characterised by recession, political upheaval and conflicts in many parts of the world. After the Gulf War, which had a disastrous impact on all sectors of business tourism, the world's travel and tourism industry looked anxiously for signs of a revival in the market. But recovery was inhibited by the recession, which was much more stubborn than anticipated.

There were important shifts in *consumption patterns*, as the clients of the business travel industry came under increasing pressure to reduce their costs and use their travel budgets more effectively.

The dilemma for hotels, airlines and other suppliers to the business travel market was that while there were signs of a greater *volume* of business travel, there was consistent and steady pressure by companies to reduce their travel costs. Cutting back became the order of the day. The business travel writer, David Churchill, summed up the situation as follows in the 25 September, 1992 edition of the *Financial Times*:

> In the heady days of the late 1980s, nothing was apparently too good for the business traveller as he (or she) forged new business overseas. But in

the harsher business world of the 1990s, business executives are increasingly told by their companies that they must fly at the back of the aeroplane, stay in a (not that convenient or comfortable) four-star rather than five-star hotel, and drive a smaller hire car.

A MORI and Wagon-lits Travel telephone survey conducted in September 1992 was one of the first to quantify these cut-backs. Three hundred business travel bookers and 100 decision makers from a wide range of companies were interviewed, and their responses made sobering reading for those working in the business tourism industry.

- 49% of decision makers said that their companies had tightened their belts and downgraded in class of travel or hotel.

- Nearly 30% of bookers working in companies with a formal travel policy admitted that it was decreed that everyone should travel in the same class, regardless of position.

- 38% of bookers believed that their companies were making fewer business trips.

This clearly demonstrates a basic principle of business tourism, namely that the fortunes of this industry follow very closely the fortunes of the economy as a whole. As recovery sets in, the business tourism industry should once again take its place as a major sector of economic activity.

What are the other trends which are set to shape the business tourism industry in the years ahead?

Advances in technology

Great advances in transport, conference and communications technology are creating new opportunities for improvements in speed and efficiency throughout this industry. The advent of computer reservations systems (see Chapter 7) has already revolutionised the business retail travel trade, while progress in the transport field has meant improvements in speed and comfort. Teleconferencing – two-way video conference link-ups – which looked, during the Gulf War, as though it might pose a long-term threat to the traditional conference industry, has found its place there as a complementary adjunct. Teleconferencing technology can be used to beam in the image of an important delegate or speaker who is unable to travel to the event in person; but the social and informal side of the conference experience is too important to be replaced by a television monitor.

Political and economic changes

Changes in the world's political and economic composition will continue to have a major impact on businesses and business travel: for example, the opening up of Eastern Europe has created a great surge in travel to and from that region for business-related purposes. At the same time, Europe's traditional domination of the international conference scene is coming under increasing pressure from attractive new destinations in South-East Asia, as that region reaches economic maturity. For the future, the completion of the General Agreement on Tariffs and Trade (GATT) may hold the best hopes for a revival of the fortunes of the world's business tourism industry. The upsurge in world trade which this will bring will have the result of providing the international business travel industry with the boost it needs to put it back on the road to recovery.

Questions

1 How does business tourism differ from leisure tourism?

2 What particular advantages does business tourism bring to the destinations where it takes place?

3 What techniques does the British Tourist Authority use in order to promote the UK as a business tourism destination?

Assignments

1 Most cities, regions and countries have a Visitor and Convention Bureau or a tourist office with a business travel department. These produce promotional material such as brochures, guides and videos, to persuade conference planners and those who organise exhibitions or incentive travel to choose these places as business tourism destinations.

Contact your local, regional or national tourist office and request some examples of such promotional materials. (If this is a group assignment, then no more than one person should approach any organisation. This will avoid tourist offices being inundated with identical enquiries.)

How does the business tourism promotional material differ from promotional material produced to attract holidaymakers? What features of the destination are emphasised in order to make it attractive to business visitors? What does the material say about, for example, the destination's transport infrastructure, the accommodation available, the possibilities for cultural or 'nightlife' excursions?

2   *Discussion topic: mixing business with pleasure*

Many travel and tourism-related businesses cater for both business and leisure tourists. Hotels, for example, often have guests from both categories, and most forms of transport carry businesspeople as well as passengers on leisure trips.

Think of how the needs and motivations of business and leisure tourists are different from each other. What problems might arise from putting the two types of tourist together? How do businesses deal with the potentially conflicting needs of both types of customer?

Key terms

Before moving on to the next chapter, make sure you understand the meaning of the following terms:

General business travel

Trade fairs and exhibitions

Incentive travel

Accompanying persons

Non-discretionary

Visitor and Convention Bureau

EIBTM

2

....

The meetings industry

- *Members of the American Bar Association are lawyers practising in the USA. In 1989, 20,000 of them came to London for their annual conference, most of them accompanied by their spouses. After a week of speeches, formal dinners and excursions to local tourist attractions, they had spent $60 million.*

- *In 1993, Lotus, the software giant, chose Cyprus for its four-day annual sales meeting for 420 sales staff, from New Zealand, South Africa, Japan and Europe. To get the delegates to the venue, 639 different flight movements had to be organised and three 5-star hotels were used to accommodate them.*

DEFINITIONS

For the purposes of the business tourism industry, a meeting is an organised event which brings people together to discuss a topic of shared interest. The purpose of the meeting may be commercial or non-commercial; the meeting may be attended by half a dozen people or by many hundreds; it may last a few hours or a week. But the essential characteristic which makes a meeting qualify as part of the business tourism market is that it engages some of the services of the tourism industry, and this usually means being held away from the premises of the company or organisation running it.

For example, a half-day meeting attended by a dozen managers who need to discuss their sales strategy becomes part of the business tourism market if it is held in a conference room booked in a local hotel, possibly accompanied by lunch. The same meeting held in a meeting room in the managers' place of employment would not count as a part of the tourism industry, as it would not engage any of the services of that industry.

The degree to which different meetings draw upon the services of the tourism industry varies widely. In the above example, only the hotel and catering sector is involved. But for major meetings, events lasting several days and requiring delegates to travel extensively in order to attend, the demands made upon the many sectors of the tourism industry can be enormous. Transport, accommodation, the retail travel trade, tourist guides, even tourist attractions and leisure services can all benefit from events of this kind.

Consider the following example. The IAPH's (International Association of Ports and Harbours) 18th world conference was held on 17–23 April 1993 at the Hilton Hotel, Sydney, Australia. It was attended by several hundred ports managers from all over the world, many of whom used the event as an opportunity to take their spouses to Australia, thereby mixing business with pleasure.

The part played by the tourism industry in providing the many elements which went into this major meetings event may be deduced from the conference programme as shown in Figure 2.1.

To the list of the many local hotels and tourist attractions whose services were used, must be added the transport companies: not only the international airlines which brought the delegates and their spouses to Australia, but also the local companies which transported them around Sydney and the locality. It is easy to understand why meetings such as this constitute one of the most vitally important markets for business tourism.

Organised meetings take many forms and go by many different names: conferences, seminars, congresses . . . the terminology of meetings is far from transparent. Even within the business tourism industry itself, there is much confusion over terminology, when discussing different types of meeting. One attempt to define the various terms is shown in Figure 2.2, which gives the definitions suggested by the tourism and leisure consultancy services, Coopers and Lybrand Deloitte in the introduction to their report, *UK Conference Market Survey 1990*.

Date	Time	Business	Social	Tours for Accompanying Persons
Saturday 17 April	Morning	Committee meetings	Registration	
	Afternoon	Committee meetings		
	Evening		Welcome cocktails for early arrivals	
Sunday 18 April	Morning	Committee meetings	Registration continues	City tour
	Afternoon	Committee meetings		Northern beaches
	Evening		Opening ceremony IAPH reception Dinner cruise Sydney Harbour	
Monday 19 April	Morning	Keynote address 1st plenary		City tour
	Afternoon	Trade exhibition opening Working session no.1		Northern beaches Coffee cruise
	Evening		Cocktails – Maritime Museum	
Tuesday 20 April	Morning	Working session no.2		Bush walk
	Afternoon	Working session no.3		Blue Mountains Art gallery and Paddington tour
	Evening		Australiana evening and bush dance	

Figure 2.1 Programme of the 1993 IAPH Conference, Sydney Hilton Hotel

Date	Time	Business	Social	Tours for Accompanying Persons
Wednesday 21 April	Morning			
	Afternoon	Technical tour to Newcastle Harbour, Kooragang coal terminal and the Hunter Valley		
	Evening		Free	
Thursday 22 April	Morning	Working session no.4		Coffee cruise
				Shopping tour
	Afternoon	Working session no.5		Blue Mountains
	Evening		Free	
Friday 23 April	Morning	Working session no.6		Bush walk
	Afternoon	2nd plenary and closing ceremony		Historic houses
	Evening		Gala dinner	

Figure 2.1 Continued

Meeting   a coming together of people for a common purpose.

Conference   a formal interchange of views or a meeting of people for the discussion of matters of common concern.

Summit   a conference of highest-level officials: for example, heads of government.

Assembly   a company of people gathered for deliberation, worship or entertainment.

Convention   an assembly of people meeting for a common purpose, especially a meeting of the delegates of a political party for the purposes of formulating policies and selecting candidates for office.

Congress   a formal meeting of delegates for discussion, especially of persons belonging to a particular body or engaged in special studies.

Symposium   a convivial party with music and conversation or a formal meeting at which several specialists deliver short addresses on a topic or related topics.

Colloquium   a meeting at which academic specialists deliver addresses on a topic and answer questions relating to it.

Conclave   a private meeting or secret assembly.

Figure 2.2   Some definitions of different types of organised meeting

THE SUPPLIERS

The principal suppliers in the conference and meetings industry are those providing meetings facilities for the market.

The UK possesses a wide choice of facilities for the hosting of meetings, large and small. Large, purpose-built, public funded conference centres may be the most visible suppliers of meetings facilities, but they are far from being the only ones. Civic halls, museums, theatres, castles, ships, and even theme parks are all capable of being used as meetings venues – often for events which use an unusual venue to make them memorable.

But, in the UK, it is hotels which have always taken the lion's share of the meetings business, due to the sheer number of small-to-medium-sized events which they are well-suited to accommodate. Figure 2.3 shows a typical conference room in a small-to-medium-sized hotel. But hotels' dominance of the market is being increasingly challenged by

Figure 2.3   A typical hotel conference room
Source: The Galapagos Inn

other types of venue. For example, the universities, hungry for additional income, have invested in year-round, high-quality products, often using upgraded halls of residence for on-the-spot accommodation. Stately homes, too, have more recently entered the market, offering rare and exclusive settings for conferences. Both of these relative newcomers are effectively eating away at the market share traditionally held by hotels.

How is the total volume of UK conference business divided up between the various types of facility? Figure 2.4 gives the answer, showing the dominance of the hotel sector.

Although, as Figure 2.4 shows, only 6.7 per cent of all venues' conferences had more than 200 delegates, it is events of this size which bring important benefits to the destinations in which they are held. Purpose-built conference centres are constructed with this market in mind. Most of them are financed through public funds and venture capital, and although few of them make big profits, the contribution to the local economy is significant when hundreds of delegates arrive to spend several days in a city. Edinburgh is one of the latest cities to build a new conference centre to attract major events.

Average no. of delegates	0–20	21–50	51–100	101–200	201–300	301–500	500
Venues				%			
Purpose-built conference centres	24.8	33.4	15.8	16.8	5.6	3.3	0.3
Large luxury hotels	22.7	30.8	25.3	15.2	3.5	1.6	0.9
Country house hotels	60.1	30.1	7.0	2.4	0.4	0	0
Other hotels	50.2	33.7	12.0	3.2	0.7	0.1	0.1
Educational establishments	6.1	21.0	26.2	21.3	16.7	3.4	5.3
Management training centres	43.9	20.6	11.7	8.1	1.9	8.8	5.0
Total, all venues	40.7	30.7	14.2	7.7	3.3	2.1	1.3

Figure 2.4 How UK conference business is divided up
Coopers Deloitte's *UK Conference Market Survey 1990*

. . . .

CASE STUDY

The Edinburgh International Conference Centre

Edinburgh's reputation as host to major global events such as the Edinburgh International Festival, the International Science Festival, the Military Tattoo and the European Council Meeting is to be further enhanced by the development of the Edinburgh International Conference Centre (EICC).

The construction of the purpose-built EICC began in March 1993, with completion set for Autumn 1995. This £38 million development is a joint project financed by the Edinburgh District Council and Lothian and Edinburgh Enterprise Limited. When completed, it will provide international standard meeting facilities of the highest quality right in the heart of Scotland's capital city. The EICC is being built on part of a 9-acre site in the centre of Edinburgh, which will be the city's new international financial centre and business district. The site is next to the Sheraton Hotel, which underwent a £6.5 million refurbishment in 1993.

The unique feature of the EICC, designed with the needs of the conference organiser in mind, is the main auditorium. Providing seating for 1,200 delegates, theatre-style, the main auditorium can be subdivided, in a matter of moments, into three separate, self-contained auditoria for 600, 300 and

Figure 2.5   An artist's impression of the EICC
Source: The Edinburgh International Conference Centre

300 delegates. When subdivided in this way, each of the three auditoria will have its own projection, lighting and sound reinforcement systems and control booth. Other features of the main auditorium level include:

● Simultaneous interpretation booths for multiple languages.

● A main stage of 200 square metres and secondary stages of 20 square metres each.

● Disabled access.

● TV and media cable ducts and camera positions.

Supported by spacious, well-appointed foyers, exhibition and catering areas and a range of breakout rooms, the EICC will also offer the latest in presentation and communications technology.

By 1993, the EICC already had twelve major conference bookings reaching into the 21st century, with the numbers of delegates ranging from 600 to over 3,000. These included international events such as the European Conference on Optical Communications and the International Congress of Diatetics.

An artist's impression of the EICC is shown in Figure 2.5.

The reference in the above Case Study to 'theatre-style' seating is a technical description of one of the several different layouts of seating possible for a conference. It is the most common arrangement of seating for such events, but by no means the only one used. The layout for a company board meeting, for example, would normally, as the name suggests, use a boardroom-style arrangement. The various possibilities and their technical names are given in Figure 2.6.

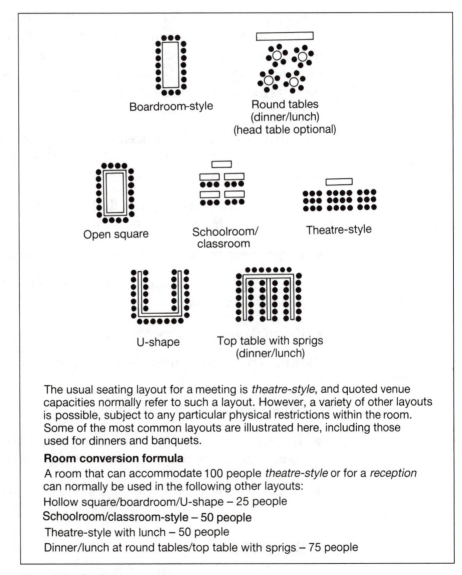

Boardroom-style

Round tables
(dinner/lunch)
(head table optional)

Open square

Schoolroom/
classroom

Theatre-style

U-shape

Top table with sprigs
(dinner/lunch)

The usual seating layout for a meeting is *theatre-style*, and quoted venue capacities normally refer to such a layout. However, a variety of other layouts is possible, subject to any particular physical restrictions within the room. Some of the most common layouts are illustrated here, including those used for dinners and banquets.

Room conversion formula

A room that can accommodate 100 people *theatre-style* or for a *reception* can normally be used in the following other layouts:

Hollow square/boardroom/U-shape – 25 people

Schoolroom/classroom-style – 50 people

Theatre-style with lunch – 50 people

Dinner/lunch at round tables/top table with sprigs – 75 people

Figure 2.6   Seating layouts
Source: The British Association of Conference Towns

THE MEETINGS INDUSTRY ASSOCIATION

The Meetings Industry Association (MIA) is the professional organisation for the meetings industry in the UK. Founded in 1990, it has some 160 members representing all aspects of the meetings industry. These members are companies involved in planning, managing and supplying services to the meetings market.

The MIA meets the needs of its members through providing education and training facilities, offering a forum and a corporate voice on issues of common concern, and negotiating business benefits. It states its mission as follows: 'to be the recognised professional body of the meetings industry in the UK, dedicated to encouraging excellence and ensuring ethical standards'.

In its early years, the MIA concentrated on the development of professional services for the meetings industry. Here are some examples of the MIA's achievements so far:

● Research commissioned with the QEII Centre and others on 'How Conference Organisers Choose Meetings Venues'.

● Introduction of a Code of Professional Conduct.

● Paper published on the legal implications of contracts between buyers and suppliers.

● Quarterly research surveys – reported in MIA Newsletters.

The MIA's plans for future activities include:

● Working with the ABTA National Training Board to set up standards for meetings industry NVQs.

● The provision of consultancy services at discounted rates for members, on meetings marketing, research, interior design and customer care.

● A review of the practices and protocols on deposit payments.

THE BUYERS

The market for the meetings industry may be divided into two main market sectors: the corporate sector and associations.

The corporate sector

This consists of companies whose main reasons for holding meetings are commercial: sales and marketing conferences to discuss strategy, new product launches, and also training sessions for staff. The main advantage of companies holding such meetings away from the delegates' normal place of work is that those attending can escape from the ringing telephones and interruptions of everyday working life and concentrate on the issues and challenges which confront them. The leisure activities which usually accompany conferences allow colleagues to relax together and perhaps create a better team spirit, away from the stresses of the workplace.

Professional and voluntary associations

Associations take two main forms: *professional*, when the reason for members joining concerns their working life, and *voluntary*. Voluntary associations cover the entire range of human experience outside working life: people's leisure activities and interests, their faith, beliefs and ethical dimensions, for example. Associations can be local, regional, national or international in the range of their membership. However widely dispersed their members, all associations need to meet regularly to bring themselves up to date with developments in their specialist field or make decisions representative of the membership. Naturally, international associations' conferences involve a greater travel element than national or regional associations' meetings. They usually involve a larger number of delegates, and also tend to be longer, since, as a general rule, they are less frequent. Competition among destinations for these international conferences or congresses is therefore extremely fierce. Fortunately for the tourism industry, the number of international associations is vast and growing, as professional activity in particular becomes more and more specialised.

An idea of the highly specialised nature of some professional associations is given by this extract from a list of clients for whom members of the International Association of Professional Congress Organisers (see page 35) have organised events:

International Advertising Association
International Aerosol Association
International Apparel Federation

International Asbestos Association
International Association of Allergology
International Association of Applied Psychology
International Association of Arson Investigators
International Association for Bridge and Structural Engineers
International Association of Consulting Actuaries
International Association of Dermatology
International Association for the Distribution of Food
International Association of Lawyers
International Association of Lighthouse Authorities
International Association of Logopedics and Phoniatrics

WHO ORGANISES MEETINGS?

With such an array of venues to choose from, who are the people within companies or associations who have the responsibility for organising meetings and deciding where they will be held?

For small-to-medium-sized companies with only the occasional need to hold a meeting, the main buyers of meeting space in venues tend to be sales and marketing managers or personnel and training managers; while within associations, administrators or general secretaries are most often the decision makers when it comes to choosing a venue.

But very few of these people organise meetings as a full-time job. The vast majority of them have to cope with the complicated task of arranging meetings on top of their normal duties. For many, this is a chore they could well do without.

Corporate organisers

Many large businesses who frequently hold meetings for various purposes have their own corporate organisers. These are employees of the company who work on its behalf, selecting and booking venues and taking care of all the arrangements surrounding the event. For a company with 20 or more events to run every year, it is a sound policy to employ their own in-house corporate organiser whose sole job is to organise their company's annual round of sales meetings, training sessions, conferences, shareholders' meetings and so on.

Venue finding services

When a corporate organiser, or anyone else working for a company or association, is asked to organise a meeting, where can they go for assistance in finding the right venue and checking availability, if they have too little experience of doing this, or too little time to undertake this task themselves? The answer may be one of the many venue finding services (VFS) (or placement agencies as they are sometimes known) which offer precisely this service.

Their job is to find a suitable venue to match the requirements of the organiser's specifications for the event. These will include approximate location, dates, number of delegates, number of breakout rooms required, type of venue, audio-visual needs, and, of course, budget.

When the VFS has sufficient information to go on, it then comes up with a shortlist of venues which match the organiser's criteria for the conference. Most VFSs use their own databases which they search for suitable venues available on the desired dates. The best VFSs act promptly: the shortlist may be faxed or telephoned to the conference organiser on the same day as the initial enquiry was made. This will be followed up, in most cases, within three or four days, when the VFS (or the venues themselves) send their brochures to the organiser to help him/her decide.

Although their services are free to organisers, most VFSs make their money through the commission they earn on the bookings they make for venues.

The *UK Conference Market Survey 1990* by Coopers and Lybrand Deloitte reported that VFSs accounted that year for over 70 per cent of bookings made and for almost 40 per cent of the estimated delegate days booked.

The survey also revealed some interesting facts concerning how organisers choose from the shortlists of venues supplied to them by VFSs. According to the VFSs which took part in the survey, the top three criteria for organisers' venue selection are:

- being close to a motorway

- being within 1 hour of a major city

- being within 1 hour of a major airport.

Clearly, location is vitally important. Other factors, such as the provision of leisure facilities, appear well behind these criteria (in fact, the survey showed that leisure facilities are used by less than 25 per cent of delegates).

Professional events organisers

Companies and associations holding fewer than 10 meetings a year can rarely afford the luxury of having their own in-house specialist staff employed uniquely for the purpose of arranging these. For such organisations, outside help is the answer. VFSs can help identify a range of suitable venues, but that is only the first step. Where can they go if they need not only help in choosing a venue, but also assistance with the actual organising of their conferences and major meetings events?

Professional events organisers (PEOs) are specialist destination management companies who work closely with their client (the company or association paying for the event), using their specialist expertise to ensure the smooth running and success of events such as sales conferences, product launches, or international congresses.

The PEO acts as the administrator of the event, being concerned with the myriad of logistical arrangements surrounding it. What are these arrangements?

Firstly, PEOs can advise on where the event should be held. Here, they have a clear advantage over the non-specialist or even the corporate organiser working for his or her own company. Since some of the bigger PEO consultancies handle over 150 events a year, those working for them have a sound interface with a wide range of destinations. This gives them the experience and expertise they need in order to know what is likely to be the best destination and venue for their client's event. Of course, the client's own preferences must also be taken into account in the decision over where to hold the event. John Fisher, himself a PEO, emphasises this in his article on the subject in the June 1993 edition of *Meetings & Incentive Travel* magazine:

> Very often, what tips it in favour of one particular venue is fashion,
> newsworthiness, knowing the delegates, being sensitive to current
> corporate culture, or even having a good volume deal going in a certain
> property. There is, dare I say it, a modest but significant proportion of
> decisions which are based on the whim of the client or his wife, however

well-argued other destinations may be. But at least a consultancy can point out the down-sides (great hotel, pity about the service; nice destination, pity about the 06.00 hrs return departure flight, etc).

Having agreed a suitable venue with the client, the next area of expertise which an events organiser will put to work is his or her skill in planning. Juggling with the vast number of factors surrounding the planning of an event takes great powers of organisation and coordination: keeping track of which options are being held where (on hotels, conference venues, airline seats, etc.), remembering when the deposits and part payments are due, calculating how many coaches will be needed, remembering which restaurant was which in a hotel on the other side of the planet which was visited for inspection six months previously . . . the list goes on.

Side by side with the planning of the event is the managing of the information flow to delegates, a vital part of their anticipation of the event and its smooth execution. John Fisher elaborates on the importance of this aspect of the PEO's role:

> Consultants are well used to the routine and discipline of timely event communication. Joining instructions need to be done well in advance so that babysitters can be organised. They may need to be individually prepared if UK regional flights are involved, with due regard to how they are going to get home once they arrive back in the UK. Most people need to tell someone back home where they will be staying, for how long, and how to make contact. A delegate programme to leave at home makes good sense. More critically, direct access to the delegates' home details in case of an unavoidable change of programme is vital, and something a consultancy is well used to tackling.

Finally, the presence of a skilled and experienced events organiser at the actual conference is vital to its smooth running and hitch-free success. Last-minute problems need to be resolved quickly and without fuss. And the unexpected must always be expected: rain in June, an air traffic controllers' strike, a terrorist attack at an international airport, delegates who get lost, fall ill or even die – all such eventualities must be dealt with in a considered manner. And it is the PEO's job to deal with them.

International congresses are probably the most involved and demanding type of event to organise. A professional congress organiser (PCO) is a PEO specialising in this area of work. PCOs have their own international association, the IAPCO, which has established a code of

An IAPCO member will . . .

Recommend that the purpose and overall objectives of the congress are clearly defined. If the aims are not clearly stated the event cannot be effectively planned.

Advise on congress taxation liabilities and make the necessary government returns.

Prepare and submit an outline plan and preliminary programme based on the expected number of participants, the venue, the duration and date of the congress and other known facts.

Prepare and submit a draft income and expenditure budget for the congress. Expenditure will be anticipated and itemized in the light of the PCO's previous experience and knowledge.

Research and identify sources of finance by way of registration fees, sponsorship or revenue from associated trade exhibitions; assess pre-financing required and identify the source, low-interest loans being a basic requirement. The delegate registration fee can be decided only after final agreement on the budget is reached, probably after the submission of several drafts.

Undertake total financial control. Establish bank accounts for the congress, manage the income and expenditure ledgers and administer the accounts, while remaining entirely accountable to the congress committee.

Establish general and office facilities necessary to service the congress from the time it is launched until the final balance sheet is completed and approved.

Act as administrative consultant to the national congress committee in the preparation of the scientific or technical programme.

Organize the drafting, design (logos, colour schemes), printing, production in the required languages and distribution to delegates of all congress documentation, e.g. announcements, registration forms, programmes, lists of participants, books of abstracts, congress proceedings, etc.

Set up systems, computerized or manual, to administer the entire registration procedure, including the receipt and processing of registration forms, the receipt, checking, banking and accounting of delegates' registration fees and all correspondence.

Create a congress image and advise on marketing policy, mailing and choice of advertising media. Arrange for any required press and public relations campaigns, including press conferences and special promotions.

Propose appropriate communication methods to obtain maximum congress response and effect.

Make and monitor all arrangements at the venue, including negotiation of the contract. These will include the required number of meeting rooms and registration and reception facilities, with proper heating, lighting, ventilation and acoustics, and all catering arrangement.

Arrange for all on-site services at the venue including efficient public address systems, electronic message systems, audiovisual equipment, simultaneous interpretation equipment, directional signs, security procedures, stage sets, telephones, banking facilities, flowers, car parking.

Liaise, when required, with conference production companies or other specialists with skills in presentation, animation, theatre, film, TV, or state-of-the-art technology such as teleconferencing. Organize any exhibitions, trade or book displays, poster sessions or other functions to be held in conjunction with the congress.

Arrange staffing on site, including supervisors, technicians, registration and information staff, interpreters and translators.

Establish continuous multilingual staffing during the congress to ensure the smooth running of every aspect of the event, and the comfort and convenience of all participants.

Arrange an appropriate programme of social events for both delegates and their accompanying guests, and pre- or post-congress tours. The special experience of a PCO is especially valuable in this sphere.

Undertake logistical organization of technical tours.

Arrange transport where necessary for delegates, ensuring they are fully informed of these and of public transport facilities.

Act, if requested, as consultant on congress travel arrangements.

Arrange for the reservation of hotel and other required accommodation (e.g. colleges) at best available rate in several price ranges and allocate accommodation to delegates as required.

Handle all outstanding matters when the congress is over and arrange for the conference accounts to be closed, ensuring that the congress committee have the minimum of obligations once their duties at the congress are fulfilled.

Figure 2.7
Source: Reproduced by kind permission of IAPCO

conduct for PCOs and works to ensure high standards of competence among its members. The extract from the IAPCO brochure shown in Figure 2.7 gives a detailed account of the vast range of tasks undertaken by PCOs and lists the many steps which go towards creating a major meetings event.

Ground operators

The task of professional events and congress organisers would be much more difficult if they did not have the help of *ground operators*. These are the Mr Fix-its of the conference scene, the people on the spot, based at the destination, who make all the detailed arrangements go like clockwork and make all the right things happen. Ground operators' strength is that, being based at the destination, they know their region or city thoroughly. Their experience and personal contacts mean that they can easily find, for example, a reliable coach operator to transfer delegates from the airport to their hotels or a firm of caterers to serve up an open-air banquet. Ground operators are also invaluable in iden-tifying ideas for social events or spouses' programmes and taking care of all the local arrangements: a gala dinner in a medieval castle, a mini cruise on the Seine, a private, after-hours shopping expedition to Harrods – a ground operator worth their salt will be able to organise such events and make all the difference between a mediocre conference trip and a memorable one.

The Association of Conference Executives

Many corporate organisers and professional events organisers, as well as meetings facilities suppliers, are members of the Association of Conference Executives (ACE). ACE was established in 1971 as the communications centre for all of those involved in the meetings indus-try. Since then, ACE has developed into a leading professional body for those who work in this sector. ACE now has over 600 members repre-senting all aspects of the meetings industry. While these are mainly UK-based, the Association also has members from many different countries around the world.

The aims of ACE are:

● To provide a forum for the exchange of information between all those involved in the meetings industry.

- To help maintain, improve and develop standards in the industry.

- To represent the interests of the industry to government and other organisations.

- To foster good relations and the exchange of information with conference-related organisations in other countries.

- To provide help and welfare support to members.

To qualify for membership of ACE, an applicant must hold a position which requires familiarity with the planning and executing of conferences, meetings, events, courses or incentive programmes.

The Association provides a range of services to its members. These include the following.

Publications

As well as a regular newsletter, ACE publishes an annual directory of the meetings industry, *The ACE Buyers' Guide*, which contains details of a wide range of conferences, services and venues in the UK and overseas. Another ACE publication is *Meetings – Finding Somewhere Different*, aimed at the conference organiser in search of novel or unusual venues. Among the more uncommon entries are the Florence Nightingale Museum in Lambeth and the Bank of England Museum in the City of London.

Training and development courses

The Association has its own training and development programme for members. This includes a three-day practical course for new entrants to the industry, introducing them to the many aspects of conference and event management; a one-day course, 'Looking After People', which focuses on delegates' security, fire procedures and basic first aid; and practical training in dealing with the media.

Inspection visits

Throughout the year, ACE organises visits by parties of buyer members to new venues and destinations in the UK and overseas. The Association also conducts groups to selected exhibitions and trade fairs overseas.

EXHIBITIONS FOR THE MEETINGS INDUSTRY

One of the most important means of communication between venues and the conference market is the growing number of annual exhibitions which bring suppliers and buyers together under one roof. At such events, the exhibitors are the suppliers – conference venues, hotel groups and convention bureaux – and the visitors to the exhibition are potential buyers – corporate organisers, venue finding services and professional events organisers.

These major exhibitions give venues a chance to publicise their facilities, especially if they have been updating or expanding these. New venues can also make their mark with an eye-catching stand, since the conference market is one in which novelty can be an important criterion for selection. Buyers can use these events to bring themselves up-to-date on developments in venues and facilities. These events are often used, too, to finalise deals between suppliers and buyers. For example, at the 1993 International Confex exhibition, held at London's Earls Court, business was brisk right from day one of the event. This is easily the largest of the British trade shows, attracting well over 6,000 buyers from the UK and overseas in 1993. Within minutes of its opening, the Harrogate International Centre signed a deal with a major motor manufacturer seeking a prestigious venue for a product launch, while the Edinburgh Conference Centre at Heriot-Watt University confirmed bookings worth in excess of £½ million.

A calendar of the main conference exhibitions is given in Figure 2.8 overleaf.

The two June events, the Conference and Corporate Hospitality Show and Conventions and Events 93, have challenged the supremacy of Confex as the leading conference trade show in the UK, causing concern not only for Confex's organisers, but also for potential exhibitors. Many in the meetings industry are posing serious questions over the viability of holding two 'national' shows within the same 7-day period. This creates great pressure on financial and staff resources for organisations wishing to take space at both exhibitions; and, from the

1993

February

International Confex – Earls Court, London

March

Human Resources Development Week – Wembley Centre, London

British Travel Trade Fair – NEC Birmingham

May

INCENTIVE (National Incentive & Promo Exhibition) – Olympia, London

EIBTM (European Incentive, Business Travel & Meetings) Exhibition – Palexpo, Geneva

June

The Conference & Corporate Hospitality Show – G-Mex Centre, Manchester

Conventions & Events 93 – NEC Birmingham

July

The Meetings & Incentive Travel Show – QEII Conference Centre, London

Education, Training & Personnel Development Exhibition – NEC Birmingham

September

ENTERTAIN 93, Corporate Hospitality, Meetings, Travel & Sponsorship Exhibition – Earls Court, London

IT & ME Show – Chicago, USA

October

British Association of Conference Towns, CONFER – Kensington Town Hall, London

BUAC Universities' Accommodation Show – Kensington Town Hall, London

IPM Personnel & Management Services Exhibition – International Exhibition Centre, Harrogate

November

ISMM (Sales & Marketing) Conference & Exhibition 'Successful Selling 93' – ICC Birmingham

Confederation of British Industry Exhibitions & Conference – International Exhibition Centre, Harrogate

World Travel Market – Earls Court, London

Figure 2.8   Calendar of main UK conference trade shows, 1993

point of view of the three shows' organisers, it raises questions over possible clashes and the impact on visitor numbers.

PROMOTING CONFERENCE DESTINATIONS

Convention bureaux

The general role of the convention bureaux and business travel departments of local and national tourist offices was examined in Chapter 1. How do they work in the specific field of the meetings industry?

A valuable insight into the work of one, the London Convention Bureau, is given in the extract from a trade press article shown in Figure 2.9.

Convention bureaux also produce publicity materials aimed at conference organisers, they help hotels and conference centres bid for events, and they generally coordinate all the elements leading up to the decision to hold the event in that destination.

The British Tourist Authority

Overseas delegates coming to the UK to attend conferences form a small but important segment of the overseas visitor market. Some 300,000 overseas visitors came to the UK in 1990 to attend a conference, spending £180 million. The growth of business traffic has consistently outpaced that of total traffic, and the conference market has generally been ahead of business traffic as a whole.

Conference delegates represent excellent revenue for the UK. They spend more per visit (£600 in 1990) than either the average visitor of all types (£428) or even the average business visitor (£500). Another advantage of conference delegates who come to the UK from overseas is that they are more evenly spread throughout the year than holidaymakers. The seasonal distribution of conference traffic is far less peaked than that of the overseas visitor traffic as a whole – although since 1988 the third quarter has been marginally the most important of the four.

The UK's success in attracting one kind of large meetings event is shown in Figure 2.10, which contains two league tables produced by the Union of International Associations.

. . . Behind the capital's success is the professionalism of the London Convention Bureau, which promotes London throughout the world with a skill that would be admired by those who sit in the boardrooms of leading retailers.

Its North American sales executive, Barbara Boyle, spends more than three months every year travelling coast to coast throughout the US and Canada, attending industry events and calling on associations, corporations and travel trade executives. Her opposite number in Europe, Juliane Lister, mirrors these activities by visiting potential clients, attending trade events and workshops, as well as co-ordinating the Bureau's own promotions on this side of the Atlantic.

Bureau head Catriona Campbell told me: 'We will co-ordinate all arrangements for event planners, make appointments for them at hotels and introduce them to professional conference organisers, caterers, exhibition consultants and any other specialist they may need.

'When a foreign organisation plans a meeting in London, and wants to involve a similar association in Britain, we will find out who they should contact. During the past few years, this is a service which we have provided for monumental masons and insurance brokers, as well as building contractors and oil marketeers.

'Many international organisations require an invitation from a national organisation before they can consider a destination for their congress or convention. The Bureau has a department that will identify suitable venues, including hotels, as well as suggesting professional conference organisers who can handle the event. We are also ready to help in the preparation of bid and presentation documents for the British association to present to its international colleagues. This may not only include a dossier of comprehensive facts and figures, but details of London's historical highlights, and letters from civic or government leaders.'

Whatever the size of the event, the London Convention Bureau is prepared to hold the hand of any newcomer. In the past, they have helped find venues for small sales conferences, linked conferences and exhibitions, product launches, receptions, banquets and press conferences.

Most of these services are duplicated in other towns and cities throughout the UK.

Figure 2.9 The work of the London Convention Bureau
Source: The British Tourist Authority, *Horizons*

This shows that the UK is in the top three countries in the worldwide league of international congress destinations, and London (which attracts about two-thirds of the UK's overseas conference visitor traffic and expenditure) is second only to Paris in the worldwide city league. How is this success achieved?

The BTA Business Travel department is instrumental in persuading many associations and companies to hold their meetings in the UK. Working with the suppliers and buyers, the following techniques are used.

Where did the international congresses go? (countries)

1988		1989		1990	
USA	881	USA	973	USA	894
UK	750	France	734	France	757
France	693	UK	700	UK	722
W Germany	488	W Germany	505	Germany	505
Italy	392	Netherlands	367	Netherlands	385
Australia	340	Italy	344	Italy	332
Netherlands	333	Switzerland	292	Switzerland	318
Switzerland	305	Belgium	284	Belgium	303
Belgium	279	Spain	273	Spain	294
Spain	276	Austria	199	Japan	266

Where did the international congresses go? (cities)

1988		1989		1990	
Paris	324	Paris	388	Paris	361
London	268	London	261	London	268
Madrid	169	Geneva	170	Brussels	194
Brussels	159	Brussels	165	Vienna	177
Geneva	152	West Berlin	160	Geneva	166
West Berlin	141	Madrid	139	Berlin	166
Rome	122	Vienna	120	Madrid	166
Sydney	119	Washington	120	Singapore	136
Singapore	109	Singapore	111	Amsterdam	108
Washington	97	Rome	108	Washington	101

Figure 2.10 League table of meetings
Source: Union of International Associations

Help with bids

International associations often decide upon a particular destination for their annual conference because their members in that country have made a bid to host the event. The BTA therefore helps UK affiliates of international associations with the costs of bidding for an international conference to be held in the UK and, if the bid is successful, with the promotion of the event, in order to maximise delegate attendance. Examples of items which can be subsidised by the BTA are the cost of producing and distributing print, the cost of hosting a reception or lunch, and overseas advertising.

BTA publications

The BTA offers suppliers the opportunity to advertise in two specialised brochures at minimal cost. These publications, which have multi-language introductions, are distributed to the business travel contacts of the 32 BTA overseas offices and to good prospects at business travel trade fairs. The first is *Britain: Country Conference Venues*, a directory of away-from-it-all conference venues offering delegates tranquillity, confidentiality and the opportunity to get some fresh air and outdoor exercise in between conference sessions. The other directory, *Britain: Where the Business World Meets*, covers facilities in city centres and those within reach of points of entry into the UK.

The BTA meetings and incentive travel workshop

Conference, corporate hospitality and incentive travel suppliers can participate in this event, at which they can discuss business face-to-face with invited overseas buyers from all parts of the world. Between 80 and 100 buyers are flown in from the USA, all parts of Europe, and as far afield as Australia and New Zealand to take part in the one-day workshop and in familiarisation tours arranged around the event. The workshop is a 'moveable feast' and has been organised in Edinburgh, Bath, Stratford-upon-Avon and Chester in recent years.

Familiarisation trips

The BTA organises familiarisation trips throughout the year, and these can be an excellent means of getting a venue or product known overseas. Groups of buyers or journalists interested in the conference and meetings sector are put together by the BTA's overseas offices and flown to the UK for their tour of destinations and facilities.

The British Conference and Exhibition Centres Export Council

Financially aided by the BTA, the British Conference and Exhibition Centres Export Council (BCECEC) undertakes the overseas promotion of nine of the UK's largest purpose-built conference centres. The nine centres – the Barbican, the NEC Birmingham, Bournemouth, Brighton, Glasgow, Harrogate, Nottingham, St David's Cardiff and Wembley – make up the Council with British Airways and the BTA.

The BCECEC runs its own overseas sales missions to raise the profile of UK purpose-built conference centres among potential users. A recent image-raising reception in Brussels aimed at senior representatives of international associations is a typical BCECEC marketing event.

The British Association of Conference Towns

The British Association of Conference Towns (BACT) is the professional organisation representing all the major, and many of the smaller, conference destinations in the UK. Founded in 1969, the BACT brings together local authorities, tourism associations, convention and marketing bureaux throughout the UK with the National Tourist Boards and the British Tourist Authority. Its main function is to promote Britain as a meetings destination to potential British and international clients.

While recognising that there is keen competition within the conference industry, the BACT's primary objective is to group together in a non-competitive manner, for their mutual benefit, all local authorities (or groupings of local authorities) with facilities which serve the conference sector. Membership of the BACT is open to all UK local authorities, or any Tourist Board, Convention Bureau or similar organisation authorised by a local authority to carry out conference and meetings promotion on its behalf. In April 1993, BACT members stretched from the Aberdeen Convention Bureau to the Jersey Conference Bureau, with about another 100 local authorities in between.

SCARBOROUGH

The Spa Conference Centre

Ideally situated midway between London and Edinburgh, Scarborough is less than an hour's journey time by rail from the InterCity station at York and is served by an excellent road system which provides easy access to the M1 and M62 motorway network.

The principal conference venue in the town is the Spa Complex, a majestic building of charm and character situated on the sea front in the delightful South Bay. Set in its own grounds which nowadays is often of great significance when security is an important factor in the planning process, it has three main halls, the largest having a capacity of 1975, numerous function/seminar rooms and exhibition space. There is an extensive parking area and excellent provision throughout for disabled people.

Catering is of course an all important aspect of any conference and standards at the Spa are incomparable with the highly motivated management team blending innovative thinking with the quality and personal service discerning clients now rightly expect. From refreshment breaks for teas and coffees to full scale banquets for up to 800 guests, absolute satisfaction is guaranteed.

Scarborough has a wide range of accommodation with a choice of '3 star' and '4 star' hotels situated in close proximity to the Spa, some with 'in house' conference facilities. There are also a great many smaller hotels and guest houses which specialise in the conference market and offer superb value for money.

In the North of the Borough at Whitby, the Spa Pavilion was reopened late last year having been completely rebuilt with conferences very much in mind. It is a delightful building with a bright, pleasing, modern atmosphere and really marvellous facilities. Set on the West Cliff shore-line, with breathtaking views of the sea, it is the ideal venue for meetings, seminars, exhibitions, promotional events etc.

Another reason for selecting Scarborough and Whitby is that the towns are situated in one of the loveliest parts of the country with outstanding scenery 'on the doorstep', numerous picturesque villages to explore, a multitude of visitor attractions, wonderful golf courses and other sports facilities to enjoy.

WHY NOT TAKE SOME TIME OUT AND SEE FOR YOURSELF. CONTACT KEITH NORTON FOR DETAILS OF FAMILIARISATION VISITS.

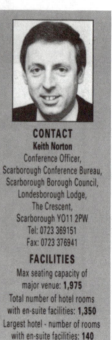

CONTACT
Keith Norton
Conference Officer,
Scarborough Conference Bureau,
Scarborough Borough Council,
Londesborough Lodge,
The Crescent,
Scarborough YO11 2PW
Tel: 0723 369151
Fax: 0723 376941

FACILITIES
Max seating capacity of
major venue: **1,975**
Total number of hotel rooms
with en-suite facilities: **1,350**
Largest hotel - number of rooms
with en-suite facilities: **140**

Figure 2.11 Example of entry in *The British Conference Destinations Directory*
Source: *The British Conference Destinations Directory 1992*

Specifically, the BACT provides for its members:

- corporate marketing activities to stimulate a greater awareness of members' activities and to offer a clearly identifiable focal point for business enquiries and leads from potential clients;

- a framework of mutual help and support;

- opportunities and systems for the exchange of experience and expertise;

- the articulation of a common voice on issues affecting the membership and on wider issues affecting the industry;

- assistance and encouragement designed to enhance professional standards, including the provision of a range of training courses;

- harmonisation of practices and agreed guidelines to avoid wasteful and unfair competition.

Among the major activities initiated by the BACT on behalf of, or in partnership with, its membership are the following.

A conference buyers' database

The BACT has developed a comprehensive database of conference and event organisers which contains detailed profiles of their meeting requirements: the average number of meetings they organise annually, the types of meeting and the average number of people involved, the times of year the meetings are held, the amount of exhibition space normally required, and so on.

As at November 1992, 7,300 buyer records (2,500 with full profiles) were held within the database. BACT members have access to the data, at discounted rates, for mailshots and other purposes. For example, a conference centre planning a familiarisation visit can use the database to select potential buyers to attend the visit.

The BACT Directory

The British Conference Destinations Directory is the Association's official handbook. Published annually, the Directory gives a narrative, pictorial and statistical summary of the facilities and attractions of each of its member destinations. The distribution of 11,000 copies to known conference buyers and organisers, both in the UK and overseas, guarantees optimum circulation to professional meetings planners. A full-page editorial entry in the Directory is *free* to BACT members. An example of such an entry is shown in Figure 2.11.

Familiarisation visits

Working in collaboration with individual members or small groups of members, the BACT organises familiarisation visits to member destinations.

The 'Confer' exhibition

The Association organises its own unique exhibition, 'Confer', currently held once a year in Kensington. Confer is the only significant trade exhibition where exhibiting is limited to conference destinations. This offers, according to the BACT, 'a superb opportunity, in a friendly yet business-like setting, for quality business to be transacted without any of the distractions of the larger, less focused events'.

Other exhibitions

The BACT has a presence at a number of exhibitions on behalf of its members. In 1993, these included International Confex at Earls Court, Human Resource Development Week at Wembley, The Conference and Corporate Hospitality Show at Manchester's G-Mex, Conventions and Events 93 at the NEC, and the Institute of Personnel Management Exhibition in Harrogate. At the International Confex exhibition, the BACT booked a corporate stand, enabling twenty of its members to share floorspace in one of the exhibition's prime locations.

Through its close links with the Business Travel Department of the BTA, the BACT can also provide its members with the latest information on the major overseas trade exhibitions and assist in the booking of space.

The press and other media

The BACT has close links with the trade press, to assist in the vigorous promotion of its members' facilities. For example, the Association has a free page of editorial in each issue of the English Tourist Board's trade publication, *Tourism Marketplace.*

Venue Location Service

The Association's free venue-finding service is a very valuable source of quality business leads for BACT members. This is open to any individual or organisation seeking a conference or exhibition venue anywhere in the UK. The Venue Location Service (VLS) is unique in being free to both the client buyer and the venue supplier – other venue-finding agencies charge a commission. It provides a central enquiry point for impartial information and advice on the thousands of available meetings venues in Britain, from conference centres, civic halls, hotels and universities to ships and stately homes. It also acts as a clearing house for the rapid circulation (normally by fax) of enquiries, matching leads to appropriate destinations via its computer database of members' facilities, thus enabling a rapid, accurate response to be made to the client. The BACT notifies selected venues whose facilities match the client's requirements, and these venues then respond directly to the client.

The VLS is promoted throughout the year in the pages of the trade press, through major conference exhibitions, and by mailshots from the BACT's own database of conference buyers. Potential buyers contacting the VLS are asked to provide a certain amount of information concerning their requirements for the event planned. By way of illustration, the following list of specifications was forwarded to the VLS in 1992 by the client, the conference organiser of the National Association of Pension Funds, who was looking for a venue for their 1995 Annual Conference and Exhibition.

CASE STUDY

The National Association of Pension Funds

Conference composition

Conference

1 Main auditorium for minimum 600 delegates.

2 Stage area for above.

3 2 × concurrent rooms for 200 and 150 delegates with enough room for small raised platforms for, say, 3 speakers, screen and lectern.

Registration

1 An area capable of taking a registration desk approximately 15 metres.

2 An area near registration for say 20 feet of message/delegate list and newspaper panels.

Exhibition/stand-up buffet lunch area/coffee and tea

1 Minimum of 1,500 square metres gross (this allows minimum of 500 gross square metres for buffet table runs) and ideally 2,000 square metres gross.

Miscellaneous rooms

1 Press office – room for 6 desks with typewriters – also room for press reception/cocktails for 50 persons.

2 Slide rehearsal room with three desks and blackout facility.

3 VIP lounge – informal seating with refreshments for 20 persons.

4 Conference office – mostly used for storage and staff breaks with refreshments for 10 persons.

5 Council lunch – sit-down silver service for 50 persons – should be accommodated in an adjoining or nearby hotel.

Accommodation

1 VIP rooms – 4/5-star hotel, 80 rooms to be booked directly with the NAPF Conference Department.

2 Delegate rooms – approximately 650 free-sale rooms of no less than 3-star quality. NAPF is happy to work with tourist board or convention bureau but would forward booking forms to delegates in house style. Ideally, all hotels should be no more than 15 minutes by coach shuttle transfer from conference centre. No more than 6 alternative conference hotels should be used.

Social programme

1 Tours – mixture of full and half-day tours for 2 days – approximately 150 accompanying persons.

2 Lunch location for accompanying persons for two days preferably in a nearby hotel for up to 60 persons, buffet style.

3 VIP dinner – in up-market location, preferably stately home or castle or equivalent for up to 100 persons.

4 Gala – either in hotel or unusual location such as museum, castle, marquee in ground of stately home – minimum of 400 persons, sit-down hot served dinner with entertainment.

Miscellaneous items

1 A number of companies offer hospitality (cocktail parties and the like) during the conference for anything from 25 to 250 persons. Such functions would be organised directly by hosting companies.

2 Coaching – we will require a highly recommended coach company to deal with transfers to and from the conference hotels and conference centre, gala evening, VIP dinner and the accompanying tours programme.

3 We would preferably also require the services of a recommended local tour operator to help with the choice of Accompanying Persons tours.

Conference dates and access times

May 1995 – last week of April or first week of May, as follows:

Set up days in main auditorium from 0900	Mon, Tues, Wed
Set up exhibition from 0800	Mon, Tues, Wed
Set up concurrent sessions rooms from 1200	Mon
then from 0900	Tues, Wed
Set up registration area from 0900	Mon, Tues, Wed
Access to conference office	Mon, Tues, Wed
Set up of all offices	Mon, Tues, Wed
Registration open	Wed pm
Conference and exhibition open 0800	Thurs, Fri
Pull out of concurrent rooms	Fri pm, out by 1700
Pull out of conference auditorium and registration	by Fri late pm
Pull out of exhibition	by Sat midday
Council lunch	Thurs
AP lunches	Thurs, Fri
AP tours	Thurs, Fri
Delegate lunch	Thurs, Fri
Champagne reception in exhibition hall	Thurs lunch time
Press cocktails	Thurs after close of conference
VIP dinner	Thurs evening
Gala evening	Fri evening
Bedrooms	Bulk arrivals Wed Bulk depart Sat Some arrivals Tues Some depart after Sat

Conclusion

Through the VLS, a successful 'marriage' was consequently arranged for this event, between the National Association of Pension Funds and the Birmingham Metropole Hotel, the venue selected by the NAPF conference organiser from the shortlist supplied to him by the VLS.

The European Federation of Conference Towns

Based in Brussels, the European Federation of Conference Towns (EFCT) has as its members the main business tourism cities of Europe. The EFCT works to maintain high standards in every aspect of European conference activity, and to achieve wider recognition of the vital importance of business tourism. It has seven main objectives:

1 To act as a focal point, making it as easy as possible for meeting-planners to arrange events in Europe.

2 To make information on European business tourism destinations and facilities widely available.

3 To assist meeting-planners to find the city or town, anywhere in Europe, that meets their particular requirements.

4 To support its own members internationally.

5 To collaborate with international authorities, associations and other institutions.

6 To undertake specialised training in aspects of conference work.

7 To act as a spokesman on behalf of the European conference industry.

The EFCT, which was founded in 1964, has over 70 members from a total of 22 countries in Western and Eastern Europe. To be eligible for membership, a town must satisfy certain strict criteria:

● It must have conference facilities for at least 300 delegates, with proper equipment and good services.

● It must have good quality hotel accommodation for at least 300 delegates.

● It must be capable of providing adequate transportation for delegates.

- It must have available a team of specialists in conference handling.

- It must be experienced in handling a number of international congresses in recent years.

- Freedom of travelling to and from the member's country must be assured.

The EFCT's main publication aimed at conference organisers is *Your Convention in Europe*. It lists basic information on each member town and is financed by the advertisements which members buy. Figure 2.12 shows the entry for Zurich.

Zürich Switzerland

Verkehrsverein Zürich
Kongressbüro
Postfach
CH-8023   Zürich
Tel. (41-1) 211 12 56
Fax (41-1) 211 39 81
Elvira Kugler-Berner
Kongressmanager

City population	360 000
Airport name/Distance to city centre/ Number of international airlines	Kloten/10 km/110
Highways	E17, N1, N3
Number of international trains daily	80

Conference Centres	Number of Meeting Halls	Maximum Capacity	Exhibition Space in m²
Kongresshaus	12	2 200	4 000
Züspa	7	20 000	35 000
Universität	89	2 700	1 200
ETH	53	6 000	1 500

Hotels	Number of Hotels	Number of bedrooms	Maximum Capacity	Banquet Capacity
★ ★ ★ ★ ★	9	1 400	4 485	3 750
★ ★ ★ ★	28	2 360	4 545	2 980
★ ★ ★	45	1 890	3 210	2 235
★ ★	14	740	—	—

Special Attractions

Zurich, the city for successful conferences! Zurich has everything a conference city needs in addition to meeting and banqueting rooms. In abundance. And it offers these facilities in a particularly charming way. Zurich features a central location, outstanding transport links, first-class hotels of all categories, enchanting vistas and outings, city-size facilities in a small-size setting, the prestige of an important trading centre and the charm of a well-kept old city. Cleanliness, safety, reliability and friendly population with excellent linguistic skills.

Participants at 600 annual conferences feel comfortable in Zurich. The affirm the host of arguments in favour of "Zurich—Metropolis Made in Switzerland", as a city for holding conferences.
Leisure facilities and sights are extremely diversified. Exclusive shopping, museums, art galleries, opera, theatre, a wide range of different restaurants and professional attention ensure a fascinating time in Zurich for all conference participants.

Figure 2.12   Example of entry from *Your Convention in Europe*
Source: The European Federation of Conference Towns Directory 92–93

Each entry contains the basic information which the conference organiser needs in order to decide if the city is a suitable destination for the event he or she is planning. A personal contact is given, usually the manager of the Convention Bureau, to whom the conference organiser may apply for further information.

CURRENT TRENDS

During the late 1980s, the UK conference market grew dramatically. In the middle of that decade, the British Tourist Authority estimated that it was worth about £1 billion a year. A 1990 survey by Coopers and Lybrand Deloitte, based on returns from 345 conference venues and 148 conference organisers, estimated that, annually, it was then worth 'considerably in excess of £6 billion, after including 25 per cent for associated travelling and production costs.' The Economist Intelligence Unit, in an analysis carried out at the same time, estimated that the total European conference market could be valued at $90 billion.

But this kind of growth was not sustained. The Gulf War threw worldwide meetings activity abruptly into reverse, as companies instructed their executives to keep their feet firmly upon the ground. And even with the return of peace in the Middle East, the state of the economy in general and shrinking corporate budgets meant that conferences remained well behind their pre-1991 level. Cancelled events, and considerable reductions in average conference duration, numbers of delegates, general levels of spending, and the numbers of spouses' programmes being requested, became widespread phenomena. As a consequence of this, conditions in the UK meetings market changed rapidly, with increasing competition being created by growing capacity chasing fewer and shorter meetings.

Coopers Deloitte's *UK Conference Market Survey 1990* noted a turning point in the fortunes of the meetings industry in the UK. In the two years leading up to its publication, the following developments were already evident:

- almost 15 per cent of venues noticed a significant decrease in the number of delegates per conference, as well as the actual duration of the conferences;

- over 50 per cent of organisers noticed a significant increase in the cost-consciousness of delegates and the range of technical facilities requested.

These trends continued into the 1990s. In 1993, CCC Research was commissioned by the Meetings Industry Association, *Meetings & Incentive Travel* magazine, De Vere Hotels and Birmingham's International Convention Centre to carry out the second *UK Conference Market Survey*. Based on a sample of 300 of the UK's top companies, the survey examined venue selection trends for the corporate conference market.

Summarised in the June 1993 edition of *Meetings & Incentive Travel* magazine, the results made sobering reading for those working in the supply side of the meetings industry.

The number of corporate meetings held in 1992 was cut by 20 per cent compared with 1991, as the recession took its toll. The companies surveyed organised an average of 7.6 events throughout the year, with management conferences the most common type of meeting (35 per cent of the total) and training courses in second place (24 per cent). Sales conferences occupied third place (15 per cent) while product launches were down to 6 per cent.

Average size of meeting

Delegate numbers were predictably down, with the average of the most recently held events at 106. (However, this figure, as well as those to follow, should be assessed bearing in mind the size of the companies surveyed – they are all among the biggest in the UK.) For the bulk of the sample (41 per cent), their events involved between 50 and 99 delegates. The larger conference, with 200+ delegates, accounted for only 12 per cent of the corporate conference market.

Average duration of most recent events

The duration of events held steady, against all expectations. In the previous *UK Conference Market Survey* (1991), 66 per cent of corporate organisers had claimed that the trend towards shorter conferences would continue, but during 1992 this was not the case. The authors of the survey put forward the theory that since there were more problems around for businesses that year, they had more to talk about!

Average size of meeting

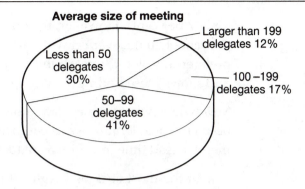

**Duration
(of most recent event)**

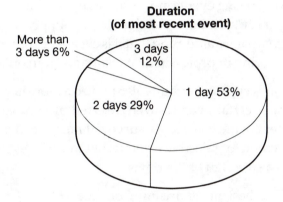

**Venues used
(for most recent event)**

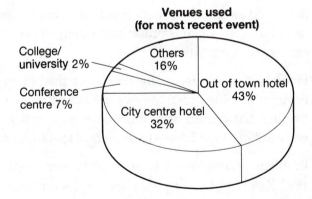

Figure 2.13   Findings of the second *UK Conference Market Survey*
Source: CCC Research for *Meetings & Incentive Travel* magazine

Venues used (for most recent events)

Given the size of events, it was perhaps predictable that purpose-built conference centres did not attract a large share of the sample surveyed (only 7 per cent). However, they did manage to attract more than 25 per cent of all the events involving more than 200 delegates. The clear preference was for hotels, which took 75 per cent of the total. Figure 2.13 shows these findings in graphic form.

Meanwhile, what venues had known all along – that lead times had been cut considerably – was confirmed by this survey. An average 6 months' lead time in 1991 was reduced to 5 months in 1992.

One of the most striking results of the survey was that professional events organisers were out of vogue in 1992. The number of companies organising events in-house was up by almost 50 per cent over 1991. The survey's authors put this down, simply, to budgetary constraints – companies assuming that it is cheaper to organise events in-house than to bring in professional consultants from outside.

Budgetary constraints also played a more important part in the reasons why certain venues were rejected by companies. In 1991, only 26 per cent of the companies surveyed mentioned price as the most common reason for rejecting a venue, but in 1992, that figure grew to 44 per cent – a sure sign of the times.

The best news arising from the *UK Conference Market Survey 1993*, however, was that half of the venues used by those surveyed were described as 'good' or 'very good', and 43 per cent of venues scored 9 or 10 out of 10 – a substantial improvement on 1991, when only 33 per cent scored so highly.

Finally, it seems from the results of this survey that the recession brought a value-for-money year, with 80 per cent of organisers confirming that venues were more open to negotiation on rates than they were in 1991. Good news for buyers, if less advantageous for suppliers.

Problems in this sector were not, of course, restricted to the UK. The 1992 *Report on Europe* published by the European Federation of Conference Towns gave the following summary of that year's developments in Europe as a conference destination:

> Competition is intense; never have conferences been more sought by host countries and cities throughout Europe. A year ago we reflected on the disastrous aftermath of the Gulf. Recovery has continued to develop, though much restrained by the recession that has affected all 28 countries represented ...

Most EFCT correspondents agree that *international congresses* remain their most sustainable market sector, though delegate numbers are restrained at present and budgets limited. Corporate meetings, more susceptible to recession, showed some evidence of recovery as 1992 ended.

To summarise, the meetings industry is lively, competitive and demanding, and has many problems. It is also essential, very profitable to host communities, exciting, and, as the survey suggests, in good hands. It continues to grow and mature; despite the occasional slings and arrows of outrageous fortune, it can be counted on to provide the new Europe with a viable, successful and profitable communications infrastructure.

The *Report on Europe* also contains a review of conference events in Europe, city by city, for 1992. The following extracts, compiled by staff of convention bureaux, provide a snapshot in time of some UK conference towns, showing them coming to terms with difficult times and anticipating the future with some optimism.

Extracts from the 1992 *Report on Europe*

Bournemouth

1990's completion of the £6 million Purbeck Hall began a chain of events that would change the image of Bournemouth as an international conference town. With larger events being hosted by the Bournemouth International Centre (BIC), Bournemouth hotels continued to invest in their own facilities in a bid to host syndicate discussions and accommodate delegates. This proved successful and has amply repaid the effort, with over 700,000 bednights recorded in the 3 years since the Purbeck Hall opened.

Despite the recession, the BIC has kept a step ahead and increased profitability by 45 per cent. A recent delegate survey showed a high degree of satisfaction with the facilities of both the BIC and the town in general. Ninety-five per cent said 'good' or 'very good', 81 per cent of delegates would recommend that their event should return to the BIC, and 65 per cent would come back as a tourist. Almost a third had an accompanying person with them, which helps increase revenue, and it is estimated that conferences contributed about £47 million to the town in 1992.

There are plans to develop the facilities still further, and this programme will ensure that the BIC and Bournemouth hotels remain long in the forefront of the international market.

Brighton

1992 was a good year on the whole, with many regular clients returning to Brighton, plus the opportunity to welcome some new clients to our town.

The new east wing extension at Brighton Centre proved a success during the first year. We opened a new conference and banqueting suite at the Grand Hotel, making it the largest such suite in a 5-star hotel outside London.

Brighton hosted the IDEA (Aerobics) convention, plus many other successful events . . .

Brighton hosted an Open Day for clients, who had an opportunity to meet with representatives from local venues and conference industry personnel. With a healthy forward diary, Brighton looks forward to welcoming back several trades union conferences, such as the TUC, NUT and others.

Eastbourne

The year has proved to be one of mixed fortunes with a small number of events no longer taking place during 1993 and 1994, while bookings for the following years of 1995 and 1996 have proved to be very strong, with increased business gained at this time. Probably the highlight of the year was when Eastbourne won its bid to host the National Association of Round Tables' 1995 event, which will attract up to 7,000 delegates, the largest conference ever to be held in the town.

Hoteliers have, in turn, held their own in a year that has seen corporate business difficult to attract, while town events have seen a reduction in the number of delegates attending meetings.

Looking to the future, work progressed well on the new 'Sovereign Harbour' marina complex which is on schedule, with the opening of the main harbour in May. This will be the largest marina on the south coast when completed; the £500 million-plus project is expected to give Eastbourne additional appeal within Europe and should add a new dimension to the incentive opportunities currently available.

Edinburgh

The highlight of Edinburgh's conference calendar for 1992 was undoubtedly the highly successful European Summit held on 11–12 December, which attracted not only the 12 European leaders and their entourages, but 2,700 media representatives. The Summit did much to reinforce Edinburgh's reputation as an international conference destination capable of hosting the most sophisticated, complex and high-profile security events.

The Edinburgh Conference Ambassadors Programme, which provides support to members of the city's academic communities in preparing and presenting bids for international association conferences, produced a total of 16 successful bids worth over £13 million in economic benefits for the city. The subjects of these conferences reflect the city's strengths in medicine, science, engineering, financial services and computing.

1992 was a good year for Edinburgh. The Convention Bureau reports a 27 per cent increase in levels of international association business and 34 per cent in the corporate meetings sector in 1992. The successful hosting of the British Airports Authority Incentive Travel Workshop in March 1992 also enhanced the city's profile in this sector, which maintained growth, despite the effects of the recession.

Glasgow

1992 proved to be the most successful year to date for conference business to Greater Glasgow. Greater Glasgow Tourist Board dealt with over 1,000 enquiries and confirmed 132 successful bids worth an estimated £25 million to the local economy. Among these were the 1995 World Science Fiction Conference and the 1997 ASTA World Congress (its first visit to the UK).

Among major infrastructure developments, the 320-bedroom Glasgow Hilton opened in November, and Glasgow International Airport opened the first phase of its multi-million pound development programme; this will allow it to cater for the vastly increased international traffic now using it. The airport serviced 4.6 million passengers in 1992, up by 12.5 per cent.

Glasgow continues to attract many medical and scientific meetings, in keeping with the city's role as a leading academic centre specialising in those fields. The future is likely to bring more pan-European meetings and offshore corporate events, but there is little evidence of this coming through yet.

London

London Convention Bureau undertook an active programme of sales trips and participation in major industry events in 1992 and recorded many successes, attracting a wide variety of events, large and small. The year ended on an optimistic note, with heightened interest from North America following their presidential election, and from Europe, helped by a favourable sterling exchange rate after Britain's withdrawal from the Exchange Rate Mechanism.

Hotel developments included Novotel's new property at Heathrow, with 178 bedrooms and meetings facilities and the Holiday Inn at King's Cross, with 405 rooms. London's Docklands saw the opening of the 440-room Britannia International with a main function room for 800 delegates and 10 smaller meeting rooms. The 95-room luxury Lanesborough Hotel, a magnificent transformation of the old St George's Hospital on Hyde Park Corner, opened at the beginning of the year, and by its end, another luxury property, the London Regent, was virtually complete; now open, it has 309 bedrooms, 10 conference and banqueting rooms and a health club.

FUTURE TRENDS

Changes in the market

What features can be expected to characterise the conference market of the future? One of the most authoritative statements on this issue came in May 1993, from Andrew Paine, President of the Meetings Industry Association. He made the following observations and predictions on the main trends in this sector:

● The market is becoming increasingly segmented by type of organisation, size, purpose, budget and delegate profile.

● The association market will see the number of European associations' conferences increase in importance at the expense of national associations. In 1990, 74 per cent of all new associations formed were European-wide in scale.

● There will be an increase in the number of association conferences discussing change, new legislation, and advances in medical and other technology.

- Size and length of events may continue to decline, as specialisation leads to the emergence of new and smaller organisations.

- The technical specifications will be more demanding for audiovisual equipment and information technology (telephone, fax, electronic mail, satellite TV) in conference rooms and bedrooms.

- Only those venues that can genuinely satisfy organisers' needs will succeed. Quality and service will be more significant than competitive rates.

- In a buyers' market, lead times will continue to fall for the smaller conferences. However, the prestigious international events will continue to book ahead to ensure the best venues.

- Suppliers will have to become more pro-active in identifying potential international association conferences and assisting national committees in their bids.

- As conferences become more participative and delegates work harder, it will be even more important to provide the right number of break-out rooms with temperature control, natural lighting, comfortable chairs and a quiet environment.

- There will be a growing demand to hold exhibitions alongside conferences.

Changes in the environment of the market

Changes can be expected in the worldwide environment in which the meetings market functions. Some of the principal trends are the following.

Competition from Asia

In marked contrast to the morosity prevalent in the European meetings industry in the recession-hit 1990s, there was a high degree of confidence in Asia, where the level of investment in new meetings facilities was extremely high. For example, of the £700 million invested in Singapore's ambitious Suntec City project, £210 million was being spent on a state-of-the-art convention and exhibition centre. In Hong Kong, £211 million was being invested in doubling the size of the Hong Kong Convention and Exhibition Centre, which was expected to result in economic benefits of the order of £600 million a year.

As Asia builds increasingly sophisticated facilities and develops stronger regional associations, the imbalance between east and west meetings will tilt increasingly towards the economic giants of that region.

Making meetings greener

As environmental considerations continue to play an important role in all fields of activity, 'green' issues will increasingly be taken into account in the meetings industry. Already, conference promoters wishing to be seen as green by their delegates are, for example, more likely to choose coastal resorts with clean beaches and hotels with good environmental records.

Meeting Planners International, the US trade association for corporate meetings planners, has its own Educational Research Foundation (ERF). In its recent report, *Trends in the Meetings Industry*, the ERF claims that meetings professionals, planners and suppliers are becoming more aware of waste at meetings, and are increasingly taking action to correct this. The ideas currently in use and recommended by the ERF include:

- printing programmes, brochures, handouts etc., on recyclable paper, and using both sides of the paper;

- using public transport or hired buses instead of cars;

- using hotels with recycling programmes in place;

- encouraging all exhibitors to use recyclable and reusable materials;

- having conference proceedings available on computer disk, to save paper.

The ERF's Resource Center publishes a list of meetings planners who are champions of green meetings.

Also in this context, three recent initiatives from the European Incentive & Business Travel & Meetings Exhibition have proved highly successful. The EIBTM *Directory of Natural Incentives and Meetings* is a manual which lists examples of suppliers reflecting 'green' considerations and buyers applying a green tinge to their events. It also features the recommended green programmes of a cross-section of professional incentive travel and meetings agencies. The second initiative is the free EIBTM checklist of 40 tips for introducing a green dimension to a product or promotion in the meetings and incentives sector. Finally, at recent EIBTM exhibitions in Geneva, free exhibition space has been given to environmental/wildlife organisations wishing to participate in the event. The aim was to reflect responsible tourism industry attitudes towards the future and to emphasise the importance of prudent promotion and well-managed development in this sector.

Making meetings more accessible

Whether there is one disabled delegate or 100 at a meeting, it is imperative that every participant at every meeting has equal access to facilities and information.

Meetings professionals can be a persuasive force in demanding that hotels and other forms of public accommodation are accessible to people with disabilities. The MPI Educational Research Foundation recommends meetings professionals to check for the following during their site inspections:

- accessibility to the venue

- ramps, lowered kerbs, for wheelchair access

- widened doorways

- grab-bars in toilets

- raised letters or braille on lift control panels

- assisted hearing devices

- closed-caption decoders

- emergency alarm systems for disabled people.

The MPI also advises meetings professionals to provide the following services:

- removing several seats from the aisles of front and middle rows of the meeting-room set-up, in order to accommodate delegates in wheelchairs;

- widening aisles at exhibitions for wheelchair access;

- including a disabled-room category on registration forms;

- preparing a list of organisations and individuals to contact when delegates with disabilities register for a meeting.

More women delegates

In 1992, the Meetings Industry Association made a call for more consideration of the needs of women conference delegates, notably in respect of security and healthier meal options. This followed research carried out by Elizabeth Peacock MP, who is parliamentary consultant to the MIA. Some of the findings of her research are given in Chapter 6, since most of them related to the provision of accommodation and catering.

A surprise finding of the survey, however, was the marked increase in recent years in the proportion of women delegates attending meetings. Figure 2.14 gives the changes in percentages of women delegates attending different kinds of meeting, with projections for 1995.

	1988	1992	1995*
Training courses	15%	35%	45%
Sales events	11%	25%	39%
Product launches	10%	29%	42%
Director-level meetings	1%	5%	15%

* projections

Figure 2.14   Percentages of women delegates, 1988–95
Source: Meetings Industry Association

Questions   1 What criteria are important to conference organisers in the
                 selection of a venue?

              2 How do conference trade shows and exhibitions assist suppliers
                 and buyers of conference venues?

              3 How does the British Tourist Authority work to bring conferences
                 to the UK?

Assignments 1 Obtain the programmes of a number of large conferences by
                  contacting the organisers. The trade press is one source of news of
                  forthcoming conferences, as is the *Financial Times*, which
                  publishes a list once a week.

                  Using the details contained in the information for each
                  conference, draw up a chart showing the involvement of different
                  companies and organisations, sector by sector: transport
                  companies, accommodation providers, tourist attractions, tourist
                  guides, shopping facilities, and so on.

               2 Put yourself in the role of the conference organiser with
                  responsibility for putting together the 'Accompanying Persons'
                  Programme for the following event to be held in your town: 150
                  American ex-servicemen who were stationed in your town
                  during the Second World War are to hold a one-week reunion
                  there in the Spring. Most of them will be accompanied by their
                  wives.

                  It is your job to organise a programme of tours and activities for
                  the wives. Think of which local excursions would be the most
                  suitable for this group. You should also consider the timing of the
                  tours, the transport you would choose, and the need for meals
                  and rest stops.

Key terms   Before moving on to the next chapter, make sure you understand the
                     meaning of the following terms:

                     Purpose-built conference centres

                     Professional and voluntary associations

                     Corporate organisers

                     Venue finding services

                     Professional events organisers

                     Ground operators

3

Incentive travel

- *Six people fly, with their spouses, from the UK to Miami, where they join a luxury cruise ship. For the following week, they sail around the Caribbean, spending each day visiting a different port of call. Their daytime activities range from golf tournaments and scuba diving lessons to shopping and organised excursions to places of interest. Evening entertainment on board includes an international cabaret, a Shakespeare play, a disco and a dinner with the captain.*

- *A family of four takes the Channel Tunnel TGV train to the Euro Disney Resort and spends the weekend there, staying in the prestigious Magic Kingdom Hotel and visiting the five themed areas of the park, from Main Street, USA to Discoveryland. On the Sunday, they are driven in a vintage French car to Versailles, where they take a hot-air balloon ride over the famous palace.*

- *At London's Victoria station, a dozen colleagues embark upon a carriage exclusively reserved for them on the Venice Simplon Orient Express. They are served a sumptuous dinner by attentive staff in the splendour and comfort of the train's luxurious surroundings. The following day, as the train passes through the breathtaking scenery of the Austrian Alps, the red carpet treatment goes on. Later that day, when they arrive in Venice, the passengers are transported up the Grand Canal by gondoliers to a gala dinner at the five-star Excelsior Hotel, before finally flying back to London.*

To the casual observer, the above trips, with their emphasis on pleasure and excitement, would appear to have no connection whatsoever with the world of business and the participants' working life. Yet each one is an example of what is known as *incentive travel*, which has everything to do with the world of hard work, ambitious business objectives and fierce competitiveness.

These are not simple holidays for the fortunate participants: not only are their employers paying for the trips in each case, but the purpose which lies behind the trips also distinguishes them completely from pure leisure tourism. For the participants or, as they are more accurately known, 'award winners', the trips are hard-earned rewards for specific achievements or incitements towards the attainment of explicit business objectives in the future. Behind the champagne breakfast aboard the Orient Express may lie many months of hard work, selling more tractors or life insurance policies or tranquillisers than one's fellow sales managers.

DEFINITION OF INCENTIVE TRAVEL

Incentive travel is as much a specialist management technique for achieving results as it is a sector of the travel industry. It is a technique based on offering travel and recreational experiences as a motivational tool to reward employees or to encourage them to meet challenging objectives. In this way, incentive Travel is most often used by companies to boost the marketing, productivity, or sales performance of their employees.

There is no consensus on a precise definition of incentive travel, but the New York-based Society of Incentive Travel Executives offers the following:

> A modern management tool used to accomplish uncommon business goals by awarding participants an extraordinary travel experience upon their attainment of their share of these goals.

From the tourism industry's point of view, incentive trips represent a distinctive form of business tourism, since they are not only planned, organised and promoted by the tourist's employer, but also financed by the employer, for business motives. However, precisely because it has the appearance of leisure tourism, incentive travel is the most invisible sector of business tourism. Very few reliable statistics are available with regard to either the size or the value of this important sector, which, for several reasons, are very difficult to quantify:

- Although statistics on UK residents travelling abroad are grouped according to the purpose of the visit, incentive travel as such is not one of the categories. It therefore tends to get lost somewhere between 'holiday' and 'business' travel.

- Owing to the highly competitive fields in which most of the companies using incentive travel operate, many of them are reluctant to disclose their levels of spending on this item.

- Employees rewarded with incentive travel are taxed on the value of their prize. In some cases, companies absorb these tax costs, making it even more difficult to put an accurate value on the industry, since in estimating their spending on this item, firms may either include or exclude tax rebates made to winners.

- It is extremely difficult to determine at what point a meeting or conference with a strong incentive element falls under the category of incentive travel. A company which flies 20 of its managers to Hawaii for a one-week 'meeting' may, in fact, be rewarding them for some achievement by choosing such an exotic destination.

WHY DO COMPANIES AWARD INCENTIVE TRAVEL TO THEIR EMPLOYEES?

Businesses engage in incentive travel awards for a variety of reasons. The most common were listed by Gammon, White and Witt in their overview of this sector which appeared in the September 1992 edition of *Tourism Management*:

- To attain business objectives through individual and/or group targets (typical business objectives might be the increasing of sales volume or the increasing of sales of specific products, for example).

- To facilitate communications and 'networking' opportunities, particularly with company executives.

- To foster corporate culture and social interaction.

- To generate enthusiasm for the following business period.

- To foster loyalty to the company.

Why offer travel as opposed to other forms of incentive?

Before the recognition of the effectiveness of travel as an incentive, most managers would have simply given their salesforce, for example, a series of 'pep' talks or sent them a succession of memoranda to exhort them to greater effort and productivity.

Nowadays, travel is considered to be one of the best means of motivating and rewarding staff. A survey of companies published by the UK chapter of the Society of Incentive Travel Executives in 1993 showed that nearly half (48 per cent) of all respondents used incentive travel to motivate their employees. Cash ranked second (43 per cent) as the preferred incentive to offer employees, with merchandise (24 per cent) and vouchers (21 per cent) lagging behind. (The survey also revealed, however, that 19 per cent of companies offer no incentives at all.)

What makes people work harder and exert more effort to win travel than, say, cash or merchandise items? And why is incentive travel so effective in advancing company goals? In their report on this topic in the September 1992 edition of *Tourism Management*, Peter R. Ricci and Stephen M. Holland offered the following explanations:

- Unlike, for example, a colour television, which anyone can purchase (and probably has) and own for years afterwards, travel is a unique experience that cannot be stored on the shelf but must be renewed each time.

- Travel awards are perceived as highly valuable, especially by corporate employees who do not have regular access to foreign travel or lavish leisure.

- There is also the social dimension of the incentive travel experience, both in the workplace and at home. When winning employees return to their jobs with fascinating descriptions of their incentive trip, some colleagues will be stimulated to strive for goals to win the following year's trip. Social status may also be increased, because not only is the winner a 'top salesperson', but he or she may also be one of the few who have visited a particular foreign country or stayed in a medieval castle, for example. In addition, when the winner's husband or wife also goes on the trip, this can lead to greater tolerance for the long hours of extra work often worked by his or her spouse in order to achieve the award.

- Group incentive travel offers even more advantages to the company and to the individual employee. It accentuates individual accomplishments by bringing top performers together and at the same time provides an opportunity for team-building. It also enhances corporate communication and camaraderie, and creates experiences that individuals cannot achieve on their own.

THE BUYERS

A 1990 survey by consultants Touche Ross put the world demand for incentive travel at 11.3 million trips and an estimated value of $16.9 billion. These figures do not include spouses, so the actual number of people travelling on incentive trips, according to Touche Ross, was probably closer to 17–18 million per annum. The breakdown of these global figures is given in Figure 3.1.

Origin market	Domestic	International	Total*
North America	4.4	1.3	5.7
Europe	2.2	2.0	4.2
Rest of the world	1.0	0.4	1.4
Total	**7.6**	**3.7**	**11.3**

* Number of trips – millions

Figure 3.1   Estimated volume of the incentive travel market, 1989–90
Source: Touche Ross, *European Incentive Travel Survey 1990*

The importance of the US market is evident. Like so many other management techniques, incentive travel is an American invention. It is said that incentive travel began there when, in 1906, the National Cash Register Company of Dayton, Ohio awarded 70 salespeople diamond-studded pins and a free trip to company headquarters. Five years later, the winners got a free trip to New York. The destinations may have become more exotic, but the principle remains the same, as for almost a century, American companies have used travel to motivate their employees.

In Europe, incentive travel has been available for about 30 years, and Germany and the UK are the leading international incentive travel markets, as shown in Figure 3.2.

Market	Number of outbound incentive trips*	% market share
Germany	290	19
UK	277	18
Spain	178	12
Sweden	164	11
Belgium	154	10
France	115	8
Switzerland	61	4
Austria	53	4
Netherlands	53	4
Italy	39	3
Total, Western Europe	**1,508**	**100**

* Number of trips – thousands

Figure 3.2   Top ten European outbound incentive travel markets, 1990
Source: European Travel Data Centre, *European Travel Monitor*

According to the *European Travel Monitor*, the top ten European markets account for an estimated 93 per cent of the total Western European outbound incentive market; the top five, for 70 per cent. This demonstrates the immaturity of the sector in certain countries. Until the late 1980s, the UK was the leader, probably because of the market's close links with the US and the number of American companies established in the UK.

Although the European incentive travel market accounts for an estimated 50 per cent of the worldwide total, it is much younger and less well-established than that of North America. Yet, since Europeans are generally more experienced and sophisticated travellers, they tend to be more adventurous in their choice of destinations and more demanding in terms of the overall product. This does not necessarily imply five-star deluxe hotels, but rather a unique experience that could not be bought by the recipients themselves if they decided to go to the same destination for a holiday.

The Economist Intelligence Unit's report on the European Incentive Study Market, as published in *Travel & Tourism Analyst*, No. 4, 1991, suggests two other important distinctions between the North American market and that in Europe. Firstly, their research shows that Europeans are much less concerned than Americans about taking their spouses with them on incentive trips. Only 29 per cent of their trips include spouses, as compared with 70 per cent for North Americans. Secondly, incentives still tend to be seen by European companies as a reward rather than, as they are perceived by North American businesses, an overall marketing tool. The report suggested however that this attitude appeared to be slowly changing.

At the level of individual industry sectors, who are the main consumers of incentive travel? Here, whichever country is being considered, the leading generators of demand tend to come from sectors where maintaining or increasing market share depends on tough competitiveness: top buyers are the automotive and automotive components industry, and the pharmaceutical, information technology and financial services industries. Electronics, toiletries and cosmetics companies are also major consumers of incentive travel.

Senior management are the primary incentive travel reward recipients or award winners, although there is evidence of the concept expanding to include other categories of employee. Incentives aimed at companies' sales forces and dealers also exist to some extent, but this is much less marked in Europe than in the US.

WHO ORGANISES INCENTIVE TRIPS?

For many companies, coming up with the imaginative ideas and making all the detailed arrangements which go towards a successful incentive travel experience for their employees is something they prefer to leave to the professionals. Although the do-it-yourself approach – leaving all the arrangements to the company's travel manager, for example – is still prevalent, particularly in the UK, companies have a growing number of specialists in the incentive travel field to choose from if they decide to use the expertise of a consultant.

Incentive travel organisers

Companies wishing to reward or motivate their staff through incentive travel can use the services of *incentive travel organisers* (ITOs). The role of such professionals is much wider than that of a simple travel agency, which in most cases will only deal with the actual travel planning.

Professional ITOs get involved from a very early stage in the reward process, and work closely with the client company to solve marketing, productivity, sales or motivation problems through the use of travel awards.

Their contribution usually begins with an analysis of their client's business and a consideration of the types of reward which complement that business and match the aspirations of those employees selected as targets for potential rewards. Once these decisions have been made, the ITO's role becomes one of advertising the promotional programme internally, monitoring employee performance and then recognising the winners. Organising and managing the actual award trip is the final stage in this process.

Many of the detailed practical elements of the trip which take place at the destination – transfers from the airport to the hotel, excursions, banquets and so on – will be organised through the services of a ground operator, in much the same way as conference organisers make local arrangements.

In its February 1993 issue, *Conference & Incentive Travel* magazine ran a survey of UK ITOs. This showed that the profile of most incentive travel organisers is one of small companies – 53 per cent of British organisers have a staff of fewer than 20. (Although 19 per cent of companies employ more than 100 people, these tend to be large organisations, often destination management companies or incoming tour operators, for whom incentive travel forms only a small part of their total turnover.)

Companies offering these services often call themselves incentive travel houses, or simply, incentive houses. The table shown in Figure 3.3 gives details of the top five UK incentive houses in 1993.

The New York-based Society of Incentive Travel Executives, with about 2,100 members in 67 countries, is the professional association for those involved in the organising of incentive travel programmes. SITE holds training conferences, publicises incentive travel as an industry to

Company	Founded	Employees	T/O 1991	T/O 1992	IT T/O 1991	IT T/O 1992	Pre-tax profit 1991	Pre-tax profit 1992	Owner
Maritz	1974	300	36m	39m	9m	11m	n/a	n/a	Maritz Inc
Other in-house activities: DTP facilities, telephone research, motivational campaigns, in-house studio. Client base: pharmaceutical, automotive, financial services, computers, telecommunications, manufacturing. Programmes remaining in the UK: 25%. Licenses: IATA, ATOL, ABTA.									
The Marketing Organisation	1980	130	17.6m	18m	11.8m	10.6m	52,655	25,000	private
Other in-house activities: DTP facilities, telephone research, motivation campaigns, in-house studio. Client base: pharmaceutical, automotive, financial services, computers, telecommunications, manufacturing. Programmes remaining in the UK: 26.4%. Licenses: IATA, ATOL, ABTA.									
Talking Point	1980	240	51.5m	75m	2.57m	7.5m	172,000	200,000	50% by the Travel Co.
Other in-house activities: event management, conference organisation, venue finding. Client base: pharmaceutical, financial services, computers, manufacturing, electronics, food and drink Programmes remaining in the UK: 30%. Licenses: IATA, ABTA.									
Brevis Marketing services	1979	28	3m	8m	2.7m	7.2m	n/a	n/a	private
Other in-house activities: motivational campaigns, event management, conference organisation, venue finding. Client base: pharmaceutical, automotive, financial services, computers, telecommunications, manufacturing. Programmes remaining in the UK: varies each year. Licenses: IATA, ABTA, ATOL applied for.									
Purchasepoint	1968	150	23.9m	18.4m	7.5m	6.5m	1.2m	n/a	Lopex
Other in-house activities: DTP facilities, telephone research, motivational campaigns, event management. Client base: broad range of clients. Programmes remaining in the UK: 40%. Licenses: IATA, ATOL applied for.									

Figure 3.3 Top five UK incentive houses

Source: *Conference & Incentive Travel* magazine, February 1993

(Note: IT T/O = amount earned by incentive travel. T/O 1992 = projected turnover. All figures are quoted in sterling.)

both members and non-members, and certifies those organising incentive travel packages.

THE SUPPLIERS

All sectors of the tourism industry have a role to play in catering for the needs of those organising and participating in incentive trips. Transport operators, hotels, tourist attractions, guides, incoming tour operators: they all contribute to the success of an incentive trip.

With its heavy emphasis on pleasure and entertainment, incentive travel bears all the hallmarks of travel for holidays and short breaks. And, indeed, most of the suppliers to the incentive travel industry also serve the holiday market.

But there are important distinctions between the holiday market and that of incentive travel, and any supplier catering for the latter must be aware of the characteristics particular to incentive trips.

For example, hotels wishing to enter the incentive travel field must be geared up to this very demanding market, not only in terms of the quality of the physical product but, above all, in terms of *service*. (The US market in particular is very demanding in this respect.) As Susan Briggs put it in her advice to hoteliers on this topic in *Caterer & Hotelkeeper* magazine, 10 June, 1993:

> Don't make the mistake of thinking that all an incentive group needs is high room rates, a box of chocolates and a bottle of ordinary champagne. It takes creativity and imagination to justify those rates . . .

> Firstly, be sure you can deliver the goods and that your staff can be relied upon to offer a high level of service . . . Participants need to feel they're being offered something to which they wouldn't normally have access. You will need to develop a range of services and people you can contact to help you provide new experiences for incentive guests. It doesn't have to be a grand fireworks display in the grounds of your nearest stately home. It could equally be talented magicians performing at each table or a Body Shop massage/make-over . . .

> Working with incentive groups will only be lucrative if you do it well. Incentive travel can mean more work. But it is worth it. Incentive guests go away and talk about their experiences, and they and their friends may well return for another treat later on.

What, then, are the features of incentive travel which distinguish it from general holiday travel? What are the special demands of incentive trips which suppliers must satisfy and which those designing them must keep uppermost in their minds? These may be summed up as follows.

Uniqueness

No single event should be like any other. Itineraries should not be predictable, but rather, full of surprises and special events. The surprise arrival of the company's managing director by hot-air balloon, for the gala dinner, for example, would be characteristic of an incentive package.

Fantasy or exotic experiences

These should be an important part of the package. Incentive trips often include the opportunity for participants to try out novel sporting activities, such as clay-pigeon shooting, falconry or hang-gliding, for example. Major hotel chains are also adopting the fantasy concept: at the Hyatt Regency Waikoloa in Hawaii, guests are transported to their rooms by boat, via canals passing through tropically-landscaped grounds.

Exclusivity

At the end of the incentive trip, the participants should have the impression that it has given them privileged access to exclusive places and people. For example, one day could begin with a private champagne breakfast served in a specially-reserved room in Madame Tussaud's, and end with an intimate dinner hosted by a titled member of the aristocracy in his stately home.

Originality

Innovative ideas are always welcome in this sector, and suppliers and ITOs need to let their imagination run riot to come up with new ways of delighting award winners. For example, given that the incentive award winner is, almost by definition, competitive by nature, competitions and games can go down well: beach olympics programmes, racing cars, mini hovercraft races . . . the more unexpected, the better.

Attention to detail

This is vital, and the importance of impeccable service cannot be exaggerated.

However, there are many pitfalls of which operators must be aware when dealing with this market. For example, one consideration is that since incentive trips are often a form of group travel, many ITOs wish to avoid the possibility of jealousy among the award winners in the group. They are, therefore, looking for hotels with rooms of the same standard and size (sometimes even the same decoration), so that one award winner or spouse will not feel that he or she is being treated less well than another. (This renders many beautiful historic properties around Britain unsuitable for some incentive groups.)

But, no matter how hard suppliers try to satisfy the demands of the incentive travel market, they will have an uphill struggle if they happen to be located in a destination which does not meet the criteria of ITOs when it comes to selecting a country or city for the trip.

What are these criteria? The key characteristics which go towards creating a successful incentive destination are as follows:

● *Accommodation*: this must be of the highest standard, offering leisure facilities and a good supply of restaurants and bars. Conference facilities are also important, to accommodate 'incentivised meetings'.

● *Image*: this must be exclusive and/or sophisticated. There is little incentive in competing for the opportunity to visit a mass-tourism destination or one perceived as down-market.

● *Accessibility*: it should be possible to arrive at the destination by as many means of transport as possible. Ease of travelling around the destination, by coach for example, for group incentives, is also essential.

● *Attractions and activities*: these should be as varied and as distinctive as possible, since seeing and doing are important elements of incentive packages.

The most popular destinations in 1992 were, for the clients of the ITOs participating in the *Conference & Incentive Travel* magazine survey:

1 South Africa, Hong Kong, Cyprus

2 Singapore

3 Thailand, Florida, Jamaica, Brazil, East Coast US

4 Cruising, Italy, Hawaii, Monte Carlo, Spain (Expo '92, Olympic Games), Portugal.

The survey noted that, despite the perceived high cost of long-haul compared with short-haul travel, destinations in North and South America and the Far East were very popular with the UK market. It is not difficult to understand why. In reality, the cost of long-haul flights often compares favourably with air travel to continental Europe. ITOs were also finding that room rates in many major US cities were falling, due to the overexpansion in the American hotel sector in the 1980s.

The EIU survey of the previous year had stressed the importance, for the European market as a whole, of intra-European incentive travel. Within Europe, the traditional Mediterranean sun and beach resorts, particularly in France and Spain, are popular. But city destinations are frequently chosen for European short-break incentives, with London and Paris heading the list of most-visited cities.

Budget

Clearly, budget is a major factor in determining incentive destinations. The company with £1,500 per head to spend on its award winners will be able to send them to destinations which are outside the reach of those spending only half that much.

How do ITOs share out the budget allocated to them by their client companies? As a general rule, an incentive budget should be split equally between the flight, the hotel and the ground programme. With a tight budget, ITOs tend to economise on travel arrangements. The reasoning is this: instead of using up most of the budget on the elements of an incentive trip which participants take for granted – namely flights (and, arguably, accommodation) – it is better to spend money on the ground programme, since this is what people remember most – the elements of the programme that they cannot repeat on their own. The ground programme element of an incentive trip is composed of all the activities, special excursions, sports and so on, which make the participants feel privileged and which make the trip memorable. So, instead of flying the participants club class to Los Angeles, the experienced ITO will choose business class and spend the money saved on a personal tour of the Hollywood film studios given by a celebrity.

Of course, the choice of a destination depends on more than just budget: there is the profile of the group to consider, as well as where the company has taken its award winners in the past. But, in the end, the budget will always determine which options are open. The smaller the budget, the harder the ITO must work to put together a memorable event.

In destinations where the weather is good, there is often less need for a heavy social programme, and this can save on ground costs. But the profile of the group is also important when planning the amount of activities for the programme. A group of senior managers, for example, are likely to have already travelled fairly widely, and so will want more included in the ground programme than, say, their more junior colleagues, who will prefer to go further, or for longer, and have less in the ground programme.

In 1993, the journalist Charlotte Vidal-Hall surveyed some leading UK ITOs for *Conference & Incentive Travel* magazine. She asked them how far different budgets would take incentive award winners. Here are their conclusions:

For a budget of *less than £500 per head*, the general impression was that award winners would normally find themselves staying in the UK, instead of venturing overseas. Within the UK, however, the possibilities were extensive, with incentive programmes based on country house hotels, stately homes and castles being some of the examples given. Nevertheless, some ITOs claimed that overseas destinations were possible at around the £500 level. Cyprus, Malta, Tenerife, and even three days in New York were among their suggestions.

For *up to £1,000 per head,* most of Europe was within reach, as well as some of the more competitively-priced US destinations, for example the West Coast and Miami. At this level of spending, incentives based on cruises were also affordable. For example, a seven-night Caribbean cruise is well within this price range.

For *up to £1,500 a head*, incentive programmes to more exotic long-haul destinations become feasible. ITOs' suggestions included the Far East, South Africa, Latin America and even China, a new incentive destination where a five-day programme organised through the China Travel Service can cost as little as £1,100.

For *over £1,500 a head*, ITOs agreed that the possibilities were practically limitless. At this level of budget, two-centre initiative programmes, combining beach and city, become affordable; Hong Kong/Phuket, New York/Bermuda and New Orleans/Acapulco were among the suggestions given.

BRITISH TOURIST AUTHORITY ASSISTANCE IN INCENTIVE TRAVEL PROMOTION

With incentive travel being such a high-spending, up-market sector, competition between different destinations is particularly fierce. How do the promotional efforts of the BTA's Business Travel department assist UK suppliers to this market? Working through its overseas offices, the BTA undertakes a range of activities designed to promote the UK as an incentive destination. Among the more important are the following.

- *Britain's Great Incentive Planner* is an annual, four-colour directory of incentive travel facilities, including luxury and unusual venues. It is distributed via the BTA offices throughout the world, and inclusion for suppliers is on a paid-entry basis. However, the BTA reserves the right to decline or amend entries if it does not consider them suitable for the overseas incentive travel market.

- The BTA's *Meetings and Incentive Travel Workshop* is an occasion for the Business Travel department to organise a number of familiarisation tours/site inspections to incentive destinations and suppliers.

- Throughout the year, the BTA works with overseas ITOs and British destination management companies in the organising of an ongoing series of site inspections for incentive buyers. These offer an excellent opportunity to get products known at first hand by the major players in the field. Corporate hospitality facilities, such as boxes at major sporting events including Wimbledon and Ascot, are very much part of the incentive travel scene, and as such are included in many incentive travel programmes.

CASE
STUDY

VARIG Airlines and incentive travel in Brazil

Brazil is already a major incentive destination and is still growing fast in popularity. It is easy to see why the possibility of making a trip to this country provides a major motivation to potential award winners.

With its exciting and exotic image, Brazil truly lives up to its reputation as a country which, according to a popular saying, 'was blessed by God and beautified by nature'. The country's assets are summed up in the following extract from a promotional brochure on incentive trips to Brazil:

> A visit to Brazil means the unexpected discovery of a place of warm tropical sun and 5,000 miles of white-sand beaches, of coconut groves and mango trees, of music and dance, of baroque colonial towns and villages, plus impressive cities of 21st century opulence and sophistication. Brazil's allure is not only in the climate, the landscapes, and the architecture; it lies in the people themselves, whose sense of cordial hospitality and friendship creates the perfect environment for your incentive programme.

Brazil's state tourism organisation, Embratur, has a very limited overseas promotion budget. Therefore, much of the promotional activity undertaken overseas on behalf of Brazil is carried out by its national airline, VARIG. This applies to incentive travel as much as it does to travel for all leisure purposes.

Before examining the role of VARIG in promoting Brazil as an incentive destination, it is worth looking more closely at the general profile of the airline which serves a country bigger than the whole of Europe.

Starting life as a regional airline, operating only in the south of Brazil, VARIG Brazilian Airlines is now one of the world's largest national and international carriers. Its fleet is currently made up of 82 aircraft, including Boeing 737-300s and 767-300s, as well as advanced-generation Boeing 747-400s and McDonnell Douglas MD-11s.

VARIG's domestic flight network links 45 Brazilian cities, taking passengers and cargo to every corner of this vast country. Internationally, VARIG serves 42 cities in 31 different countries, providing the most comprehensive route system to Brazil of any carrier.

The main international gateways to Brazil are Rio de Janeiro and São Paulo; however, VARIG also offers an international service to and from Manaus and

Figure 3.4   VARIG Brazilian Airlines' 747–300 jet
Source: Reproduced by kind permission of VARIG/Gold Star Public Relations Ltd

Belém in the Amazon, Fortaleza, Recife and Salvador in the north-east, and Foz do Iguaçu, Florianópolis and Porto Alegre in the south.

As the principal carrier linking Brazil with the rest of the world, VARIG has an obvious interest in stimulating the demand for business travel to that country. Promoting Brazil as a destination for incentive award winners is the responsibility of a team of VARIG staff based in the company's headquarters in Rio de Janeiro. The Congress, Convention and Incentive Travel Department undertakes all of the promotional tasks normally carried out by national tourist office personnel: producing printed material on incentive travel ideas, collaborating with Brazil's top hotels, and ensuring that Brazil is represented at the principal business travel shows, such as the Incentive Travel and Meetings Exhibition in Chicago and Geneva's European Incentives, Business Travel and Meetings Show.

The airline's Rio de Janeiro staff are assisted by an international network of VARIG sales staff based in its 141 overseas offices and having special responsibility for selling to the business travel market. In VARIG's London office, it is the job of the Tours and Events Sales Manager to look after UK incentive groups heading for Brazil.

As well as advising incentive travel organisers on putting together the right destinations in Brazil for the award winners in question, VARIG's specialist staff can assist in all the planning stages right through to the last check-in before departing for Brazil.

For group incentives, the special treatment can continue even in the air. The airline can arrange special on-board recognition for incentive groups including: headrest covers imprinted with the award winners' company's logo, in-flight meal menus imprinted with the company logo, personalised welcome cards placed on award winners' food trays, and even the use of the aircraft's television system to show company videos welcoming the incentive travellers aboard.

For incentive travel organisers, VARIG provides sample itineraries, to show the major attractions which can be included in an incentive trip to Brazil. Some of the suggested itineraries for a six-day incentive trip are shown in Figure 3.5.

CURRENT TRENDS

Cost-cutting

Following the free-spending spree of the previous decade, the world-wide recession of the early 1990s brought a new air of realism to the incentive travel business. Value for money became the incentives buyer's number one criterion, and suppliers became aware of the need to compete on this basis to get the business. As a result, some very keen prices were to be had in the marketplace.

One indication of this trend was the increasing popularity of buying pre-packaged, off-the-peg incentive trips as a way of providing added value for money. Meridien, Hyatt, Ciga and Marriott were among the international hotel groups introducing packages at selected properties. These included sightseeing tours, themed dinners, entertainment and special events. Working with local destination management companies, the hotels were able to create programmes designed to suit clients' needs.

Many of these packages were being used to promote new properties or boost business at existing hotels, and so were offered at rates well below those normally available. One example was Le Meridien Porto, with a

RIO DE JANEIRO	RIO/SÃO PAULO	RIO/SALVADOR
1st Day Arrival in Rio/transfer to hotel. Welcome party at hotel/or cocktail party on Sugar Loaf. Evening: Dinner at a typical Brazilian barbecue restaurant. **2nd Day – Tour** • Visit to the Botanical Gardens • Visit to the world-famous beaches of Copacabana and Ipanema • Visit to the Imperial Palace • Visit to the Maracana Soccer Stadium • Lunch at a typical Brazilian seafood restaurant at Guanabara bay Evening: Theme party at an 18th century mansion. **3rd Day** Corcovado (statue of Christ the Redeemer) and Tijuca forest tour. Evening: Dinner and Samba show. **4th Day** Paradise Island cruise in Sepetiba bay on a typical Brazilian schooner with open bar. Visit to uninhabited islands for swimming, snorkelling or just relaxing. Lunch at St Martins island/entertainment. Night: Dinner at restaurant in Municipal theatre – formal service. **5th Day** Optional tours to Iguassu falls, Brasilia or São Paulo/or a full day in Petrópolis with lunch. Evening: 'Farewell to Rio' Carnival party, including cocktails, dinner and entertainment. **6th Day** Beaches and/or shopping. Lunch and farewell cocktail party at the hotel. Night: Transfer to airport/departure.	**1st Day** Arrival in São Paulo/transfer to hotel. Welcome lunch. Afternoon: Half day city-tour. Evening: Dinner/show at São Paulo's famous show house. **2nd Day** Tour to Simba Safari zoo (lunch included). Evening: 19th century theme party. **3rd Day** Morning at leisure. Transfer to airport/departure to Rio. Arrival in Rio/transfer to hotel, including mini-tour of beaches. Cocktail/lunch in hotel. Afternoon at leisure. Evening: Welcome cocktail party/dinner/Samba show on top of Sugar Loaf. **4th Day** Breakfast at hotel. Half day city-tour including statue of Christ the Redeemer, Tijuca forest, Barra da Tijuca with lunch at a barbecue restaurant. Afternoon at leisure. Evening: Dinner and theme party at 19th century mansion. **5th Day** Boat tour including Guanabara bay, Copacabana, Ipanema and Leblon beaches, and the Cagarras islands (lunch served on board). Evening: Farewell cocktail party/dinner/Samba show at a private club. **6th Day** Full day at leisure (beach, shopping, sports, etc.). Lunch at a traditional restaurant. Evening: Transfer to airport/departure.	**1st Day** Arrival in Rio/transfer to hotel, including mini-tour of beaches. Evening: Cocktail party and dinner. **2nd Day** Guanabara bay cruise (lunch on board). Evening: Dinner at a Brazilian typical barbecue place. **3rd Day** Departure to Salvador on an early morning flight. Arrival in Salvador/transfer to hotel for lunch. Afternoon: Historical city tour. Evening: Dinner and famous Bahian cruise. **4th Day** After breakfast in the hotel, a schooner cruise including lunch. Evening: 'Bahian night' party. **5th Day** Departure on an early morning flight to Rio. Arrival in Rio/transfer to hotel for lunch. Afternoon at leisure (shopping, tennis, golf, swimming, etc.). Evening: Farewell cocktail party on top of Sugar Loaf – dinner and live Samba show. **6th Day** Half day city-tour, Tijuca forest and statue of Christ the Redeemer. Lunch at one of Rio's fashionable lunch spots. Evening: Transfer to airport/departure.

Figure 3.5 Some sample incentive travel itineraries

three-day incentive package including a visit to the local port wine cellars (a tasting and dinner), a tram ride, boat trip and gala dinner, for £178 per person.

Most hotels' incentive packages are limited to accommodation and ground programme only, although most hotel groups could either arrange flights for clients or put them in contact with those who could make the arrangements on their behalf.

Another side-effect of the business climate of the 1990s was that pure incentive travel began losing ground to what became known as 'incentivised meetings' – companies including a minimum half-day seminar or meeting in an incentive programme, to camouflage the real nature of the trip and thus avoid incurring taxes. Another advantage of this for the company is that they can use the opportunity of having all their most prized staff or sales representatives together in one group, to give them a powerful pep-talk in order to motivate them to even greater productivity or sales success in the future.

The mood of the moment was summed up in June 1993 by Sara White, editor of *Conference & Incentive Travel*:

> In a climate of accountability and value, people are looking to offer more worthwhile incentives. Fewer companies now run incentive programmes which are pure leisure; most people try to include a business session of sorts. Buying patterns are little changed. Today's buyer is like the majority of people – searching for value. Corporate buyers are looking for quality and good prices. Other criteria, including originality and flexibility, lag far behind.

The length of an incentive trip is another variable which can be used as a cost-cutting measure. The average length of European companies' incentive trips to international destinations within Europe was estimated by Touche Ross in 1989/90 to be around five days. But a year later, in 1991, there were already signs that the average duration of a European incentive trip was declining, as companies tried to cut back on spending. An average three to four days for a short-haul destination was already the norm for this market by the early 1990s.

Long-haul destinations continued to generate longer trips, averaging eight days, and domestic incentives were still just for a couple of nights, usually at the weekend.

Another variable – the size of incentive groups – was cited by the ITOs participating in the *Conference & Incentive Travel* magazine's survey (see page 77) as being a factor used by companies to cut back on their spending on incentives.

According to the ITOs, the recession had in general meant smaller groups, particularly to long-haul destinations, although no move away from group to individual programmes was reported.

Changing destination trends

Short-haul

In its study of the European incentive market as reported in *Travel & Tourism Analyst*, No. 4, 1991, the Economist Intelligence Unit (EIU) noted, within Europe, clear evidence of an emerging trend away from Mediterranean resorts, in favour of Eastern European destinations – notably cities such as Prague and Budapest – and Scandinavia:

> Scandinavia is considered a growth destination particularly in the winter when it offers an exotic appeal, with floodlit reindeer rides, camp fire dinners and snow treks, for example.

But Eastern Europe was firmly expected to be the fastest-growing European incentive destination for a good few years ahead.

Similarly, in the Touche Ross *European Incentive Travel Survey 1990*, Eastern Europe came out clearly on top as the destination perceived as most likely to become more attractive in the future for incentive travel. This is understandable: as well as having a certain novelty value as a destination, Eastern Europe is rich in the attractions sought by many incentive groups, for example:

- fine cities, full of culture and heritage, often attractively situated on prime rivers such as the Danube, Vistula and Vltava;

- attractive scenery and tourist sites, for excursions;

- national cuisine and, in some cases, well-known national beers and wines;

- folklore, customs, distinctive music and dance;

- well-developed sports facilities;

- established spas and health resorts.

But political instability, outdated infrastructure and poor ground handling arrangements remain, in many Eastern European countries, important barriers to hosting incentive travel movements. Investment in new hotels and airport terminals and the setting up of specialised incentive divisions within national tourist organisations should address some of these problems.

Long-haul

The EIU predicted that in the short-to-medium term, short-haul destinations within Europe could benefit at the expense of more exotic long-haul trips, as companies continued to look for lower-cost alternatives. In the longer term, however, increasing competition from destinations further afield was expected to make itself felt. An upturn in economic well-being would mean that traditional resort destinations, notably Spain and the Mediterranean, would probably suffer the most, as companies buying incentives sought newer, more exclusive and unusual destinations.

In the search for novelty value, the USA's dominance as a long-haul incentive destination for Europeans could be threatened. The EIU reported that Brazil, Mexico and Canada were frequently cited by ITOs as up-and-coming destinations – both Brazil and Mexico are perceived as exotic, while Canada appeals to the more adventurous, offering a wide range of sporting activities in winter and summer.

The Far East and South-East Asia also registered good growth in the early 1990s, with Thailand, Singapore and Hong Kong among the most popular long-haul destinations quoted. With fierce price wars among the airlines and hotel rates in the Far East and the USA much lower than in many European destinations, cities such as Paris, Monaco and London face increasing competition from incentive destinations located in other continents.

Not only are the actual preferred destinations for incentive trips changing, but there are also signs that what award winners want to do during their trip is undergoing a transformation too. According to the Minneapolis-based Carlson Marketing Group, a major incentive travel marketeer, the outdoor adventure and ecotourism segments of the business are among the fastest-growing areas. These fit into the growing 'lifestyles concept' of incentive travel, where smaller groups are taken on an outdoor adventure that suits their interests, rather than chartering a plane and flying everyone to the same destination. C. Ross, the outdoor travel director at Carlson, reported to Peter R. Ricci and Stephen M. Holland (*Tourism Management*, September 1992) that there is a trend away from the resort hotel with its *haute cuisine* and jacuzzi for some segments of the incentive market, because some clients have already had enough of that. They are seeking a different quest, such as a hunting-photography safari, an Alaskan adventure, a fishing holiday on a quiet lake in an isolated setting with comfortable but rustic accommodation, or a South American rain forest trip.

New uses of incentive travel

New trends in corporate reward systems, with more emphasis on teamwork and company-wide (as opposed to individual) goals mean that growth potential for incentive travel may lie in this technique being increasingly used to motivate the broader workforce – instead of only the chosen few in 'key' positions.

The majority of respondents in the *Conference & Incentive Travel* magazine survey predicted a growth in incentives for non-sales employees (eg administration staff), with some forecasting an increase as high as 10 per cent. One ITO was quoted as saying 'All sectors of business are going to be under pressure to achieve "better results from less", and having a motivated workforce will be essential.'

The EIU report also noted a change in companies' use of incentive awards. For the UK and Germany, the EIU identified a trend towards the strategic use of incentives as a *regular* means of boosting performance and productivity, rather than as a reward for one-off competitions or projects, as had been the pattern for most companies up until the 1990s. This integration of regular incentive travel awards into the business and marketing plans of a growing number of companies is the clearest sign yet that the market has finally matured.

However, the contribution which incentive travel awards can make to companies' performance and productivity levels needs to be understood and accepted not only by senior management, but by all employees, as well as shareholders and the public as a whole.

In a tight economic situation, activities which are 'seen' to be non-essential are very vulnerable, and many onlookers may question the wisdom of a company sending 50 of its best employees on a one-week, all-expenses-paid trip to Thailand at a time when corporate belt-tightening is the order of the day. For this reason, there is a need for the benefits of incentive travel to be clearly and widely explained. It is essential that the incentive travel industry presents itself well to the corporate buyer and that the clear advantages of a travel-related reward are explained to all involved.

Questions

1 Why is it so difficult to quantify incentive travel?

2 Why do companies most often choose to reward their employees with travel, as opposed to other forms of incentive such as money?

3 What are the features of an incentive trip which distinguish it from a general leisure trip?

Assignments

1 Choose a city in your country which, in your opinion, could be a successful incentive destination (see the characteristics of such destinations on page 80). Write the text for a promotional brochure, to be distributed directly to large companies, to persuade them to consider their city for short-break incentive trips for their employees. Emphasise the aspects of the city which make it an excellent choice for this type of tourism. Add photographs and other illustrative material if possible.

2 The manager of a local hotel in your area has asked your assistance in helping him break into the incentive market for small groups. He is planning a mailshot to the major incentive houses, describing the facilities of his hotel and the possibilities for incentive activities in the locality.

He wants you to compile a list of ideas for possible activities and events for award winners staying at his hotel. What would you suggest?

You may find the following advice for hoteliers useful. It is an extract from an article by Susan Briggs in the *Caterer & Hotelkeeper* magazine of 10 June 1993, entitled, 'That special break: making incentive travel work for you':

> Possible components for incentive trips could include special openings or tours of local sights (especially if they are either quirky or famous) such as historic houses or gardens. Opportunities to try unusual sports or activities and even local crafts are also popular.

> If you are planning to offer incentive stays for smaller groups or just couples, perhaps it is worth trying to find a local celebrity or 'character' to show them around the area – guaranteeing a very personal insight and making them feel very privileged.

> Think of an incentive as a special treat for someone and let your imagination run riot to come up with incentive suggestions. What sort of thing do people dream of doing? Could you suggest a way of organising it? For example, you could make a childhood dream to be a train driver come true by contacting a local group of steam enthusiasts.

Key terms

Before moving on to the next chapter, make sure you understand the meaning of the following terms:

Award winners

Incentive travel organisers

Incentive houses

Ground programme

4

The exhibitions industry

- *The annual Paris Air Show attracts not only members of the public who travel out to the airport for the day, but more importantly several thousand potential buyers who travel to the show from all over the world. They are there with a professional interest, with a view to seeing the latest developments in the civil and military aeronautical industry and purchasing aircraft for their airline or their government.*

- *Every year in Berlin, the ITB travel trade fair is attended by some 30,000 members of the worldwide tourism industry, who attend the event in order to meet each other and exhibit their destinations to the 100,000 members of the public who visit.*

DEFINITION

Exhibitions, which may also be called shows or trade fairs, have been defined as 'presentations of products or services to an invited audience with the object of inducing a sale or informing the visitor'. In this sense, exhibitions represent a form of three-dimensional advertising where, in many instances, the product can be seen, handled, assessed by demonstration and in some cases even smelled and tasted.

As an advertising medium, exhibitions play a vital role in the marketing of goods and services. They encourage home trade, and because of the high proportion of foreign visitors attending them, they also promote exports. As a sector of the business tourism industry, exhibitions contribute to invisible earnings by attracting overseas visitors and generate wealth to the economy within the area of their location.

Exhibitions are considered part of the business tourism industry because they stimulate travel for two different groups of people: the exhibitors, who travel to the event in order to work at selling their product or service; and the exhibition visitors, who, except in the case of consumer shows, are most likely to be attending for work-related reasons: to see the latest developments in hotel kitchen equipment, farm machinery, or printing technology, for example.

Exhibitors, as well as those visiting exhibitions, create a high level of demand for travel services, catering and accommodation. Overseas visitors to trade exhibitions are among the highest-spending categories of business tourists. All sectors of the industry benefit from this particular clientele.

The total value of the exhibition business in the UK in 1991 was estimated to be £1,320 million. Figure 4.1 shows how this sum is divided up.

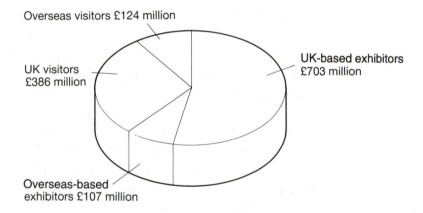

Note: These sums include: the cost of exhibitor space, stand building, staffing costs, promotional costs, food, drink, travel and hotel costs.

Figure 4.1   Breakdown of exhibition spend in the UK
Sources: ISBA, EIF 1991, research of 464 companies across a range of industrial sectors and 5,763 visitors to a cross-section of 39 events

History

Although producers and merchants have displayed their wares at fairs since pre-Biblical times, the present UK exhibition industry can trace its origin back to the first industrial exhibitions held in London in 1760 and 1791. These large-scale events were organised by the Royal Society of Arts and culminated in the Great Exhibition of 1851 which was housed in the giant 'Crystal Palace' erected in Hyde Park, London. Over six million visitors attended this event, which generated profits of over £180,000. These invested funds largely financed the development of the museums in Exhibition Road, London, the Royal Albert Hall and the Royal College of Music.

The succeeding years witnessed the building of numerous exhibition facilities in the UK – for example, Alexandra Palace and the Royal Agricultural Hall, both in 1862, Olympia in 1886, and Earls Court in 1937. Prolific investment in exhibition halls in the UK has continued up to the present day. Of particular note are the National Exhibition Centre, Birmingham, opened in February 1976, and the Wembley Exhibition Centre, opened in 1977.

TYPES OF EXHIBITION

Exhibitions may range from a multiplicity of small local displays, for example of arts and handicrafts, up to the largest agricultural shows attracting many thousands of visitors. 'Exhibition' is not a precise term. In consequence, the main professional organisations in this field are careful to define what is meant when speaking about the 'exhibition market', for example. In principle, only exhibitions which are held in recognised, dedicated venues which themselves are larger than 2,000 square metres are accorded the term 'exhibition' for the purposes of published surveys.

The majority of exhibitions in the UK fall into one of three main categories.

Agricultural shows

These are invariably held in the countryside on open sites, with a high proportion of temporary cover, and normally take place once a year. Visitor expenditure is significant, from admission charges, car parking, concession sales of refreshments, catalogues and other services. Exhibitors range from financial and agricultural support schemes and farm equipment manufacturers, to crafts and livestock display. Attendances range from 5,000 to 200,000 at the largest event within a period of one to five days.

Consumer shows

These events are aimed principally at the general public, although they may have trade aspects, on subjects of broad-ranging interest. Well-known examples are the Motor Show, Boat Show, and Ideal Home exhibitions. Extensive promotion for these exhibitions is undertaken through the media of TV, radio, press and posters. Such shows usually contain a strong element of entertainment.

Specialised trade shows and exhibitions

These are events in which the product emphasis and target buying audience are, to a large extent, defined and controlled by the organiser. It is this area of industrial, trade and technical fairs which has shown the largest individual growth pattern in the UK, where over 400 such events are now held annually. A limited number, such as fashion shows, many of which are major events, are held biannually.

Typically, some 38 per cent of exhibitions are held between March and June, and 36 per cent between September and November, the busiest seasons for such events.

THE CONFERENCE LINK

Exhibitions are increasingly accompanied by conferences or seminars as a means of promoting subject interest and as an additional information and educational benefit from attending the exhibition. Some trade and technical fairs offer a structured programme of workshops, forums and demonstration courses. These offer obvious advantages, not least in extending the media coverage – perhaps by having a celebrity speaker – and establishing the event as a 'worthwhile visit' for those attending.

Conversely, many conferences also generate a need for an associated exhibition which adds a visual and practical dimension. In many cases it also provides revenue to offset the costs of organising the conference.

It is estimated that some 20 per cent of exhibitions provide an affinity 'conference' and that a similar percentage of conferences organise 'alongside' exhibitions to accompany them. The secret of success in both concepts is allowing sufficient time within the conference programme for delegates to visit the exhibition – and for the exhibition audience to attend the seminar/workshop, without denuding the exhibition hall.

EXHIBITIONS AS A SALES MEDIUM

Exhibitions and trade shows have always been regarded as an excellent source of sales contacts and an opportunity to meet potential customers of the highest quality. This is one of the reasons why exhibitions have withstood the rigours of the recession relatively well.

Such events can be one of the most efficient ways of promoting and selling products and services, and it is for this reason that so many exhibitors travel to exhibitions in order to participate. Independent research undertaken by Taylor Nelson Business Services and the University of North London reveals that trade exhibitions have three unique qualities for exhibitors.

- Exhibitions attract dedicated and specific target audiences drawn by promotion focused on clearly identified market sectors.

- A very high proportion of visitors have buying authority.

- Exhibitions generate a high level of quality sales leads with excellent conversion to sales ratios.

The same research identified equally unique benefits for the visitor or buyer. In order of importance, these were:

1 There is a valuable opportunity to have face-to-face contact with the personnel of the company.

2 There is an important benefit in that products can be handled, seen and demonstrated.

3 There is the ability to view and compare a wide range of products at one time.

In an effort to quantify the effectiveness of exhibitions as a sales medium, the Exhibition Industry Federation (EIF) conducted a survey of 345 exhibitors in 1991. Of the exhibitors who kept detailed records, there was (not surprisingly) a wide disparity in the number of 'sales contacts' made. Some companies reported as few as 10, while others had over 1,000 from a single exhibition. This is to be expected, given the variety of companies using the exhibition medium. For a firm selling oil rigs, one sale is a tremendous success, while a giftware or clothing manufacturer would expect a major exhibition to generate many hundreds of orders.

This kind of wide divergence creates problems when it comes to producing average figures for exhibitions. For example, the EIF research indicates that companies in the engineering field estimated 'cost per visitor contact' at £41 and 'cost per sale' at £215. However, travel and tourism companies put the respective figures at £17 and £59. (This also raises the question of what is meant by a 'sale': clearly a £100 order is not a £1 million order.) Another difficulty is that many companies find it difficult to separate out the effects of a contact made at an exhibition and one made through their sales representatives or through sales presentations made elsewhere.

In the attempt to overcome the problems involved in comparative valuation, the Exhibition Marketing Group (composed of Reed, EMAP, Andry Montgomery, Blenheim, Earls Court, Olympia and the NEC) commissioned independent research in the second half of 1991 from Taylor Nelson/AGB. As part of their research 1,308 UK-based companies operating in thirteen different sectors were interviewed about their use of media and the effectiveness of those media in achieving certain objectives. The survey was based on a sample of companies known to be exhibitors in these sectors, since these companies are in the best position to comment on the effectiveness of exhibitions in relation to other media. The principal results of this survey are illustrated in Figure 4.2.

SUPPLIERS

Exhibition halls

These are the venues where exhibitions can be held. The hall owner, often referred to as 'the landlord', may be a municipal authority, property company, hotelier or even a landowner.

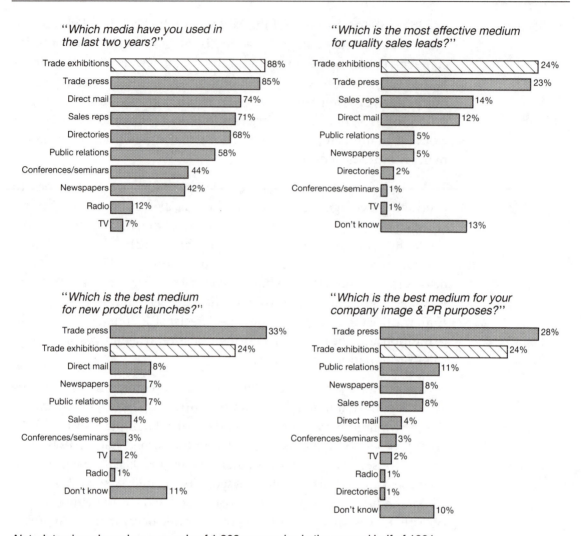

Note: Interviews based on a sample of 1,308 companies in the second half of 1991.

Figure 4.2   **Results of survey on selected UK companies' use of media**
Source: Taylor Nelson/AGB for the Exhibition Marketing Group

The role of the hall owner is normally to provide covered space with access for transport to deliver on site, visitor reception facilities, car parking, and a variety of support services ranging from catering to first-aid, and security to cleaning.

In the UK, there are 23 exhibition halls capable of holding events of at least 2,000 square metres. In 1991, there were 660 exhibitions recorded in these venues. Of these, 56 per cent were held at Birmingham's

National Exhibition Centre (NEC) and Earls Court, Olympia in London. Because of the enormous size of these events, these two exhibition centres between them were estimated to account for over 75 per cent of the total turnover of the whole industry.

The dominance of the market by the NEC and Earls Court, Olympia is obvious, and can be explained in terms of simple scale alone. The NEC has 158,000 square metres of exhibition halls and has its eyes set firmly on 200,000 square metres by the year 2000. For 1993, there were 104 exhibitions scheduled, of which 8 were new, first-time events. The Earls Court 2 exhibition centre opened in December 1990, increasing London's available exhibition space by 17,000 square metres. In 1992, it saw a 44 per cent increase in occupancy.

Exhibition organisers

Exhibition organisers are essentially 'promoters' and primary risk takers. They may be private entrepreneurs, subsidiaries of publishing houses, or trade/professional associations with a specialised interest. Increasingly, organisers adopt extensive research into the potential viability of an exhibition prior to its launch – and subsequently, when established, for its development and promotion.

An exhibition centre is licensed to an exhibition organiser for a specific period on terms negotiated between him or her and the hall owner. (Recently, some hall owners have adopted the role of exhibition organiser for the promotion of events in their own facility, to maximise the financial return on the venue.)

The organiser is responsible for the overall logistics involved in mounting the exhibition – finding participating exhibitors and publicising the event to attract, in many cases, a specialised audience. The organiser also defines and publishes regulations governing the exhibitions and exhibitors' obligations.

In addition, it is the organiser's role to:

- define the exhibition's profile – the target areas for both exhibitors and visitors;

- create the image of the exhibition, including a coined short title and a memorable symbol or logo;

- devise a theme as a coordinating thread, drawing together promotional material and displayed advertising for both space-selling and visitor attendance.

The organiser is also responsible for devising and implementing the marketing plan for the exhibition. What does this entail?

Firstly, the organiser will produce an eye-catching, space-selling brochure to distribute to potential exhibitors whose names and addresses have been trawled from a variety of sources. The brochure will contain basic details of costs, types of stand on offer, statistics of the relevant industry/market, its potential growth and the part the exhibition will play in the exhibitor's effort to capture a larger share. References will be made to the track record of previous exhibitions with audited facts and figures.

Copies of the brochure will also be sent to relevant publications with an accompanying press release defining the aims of the exhibition and its potential. Ideally, this will be supported by a displayed advertising campaign, the exercise being followed up with regular issues of press releases.

The overall marketing plan is also likely to include the production and distribution of a periodic news sheet to exhibitors, highlighting the show's progress and providing advice on maximising participation and methods of self-promotion.

Stand and service contractors

The services element of the exhibitions industry includes, in the main, stand-fitting, electrical, floor coverings, furnishings, display, freight handling, lifting, floral and cleaning. Stand and service contractors may be either nominated by the exhibition organiser – in some instances the hall owner – or engaged by the exhibitor on the basis of past experience.

Exhibitions comprise a series of 'stands', 'booths' or 'open sites'. These are either individually designed on behalf of the exhibitor or provided by the organiser as a 'modular unit' or 'shell scheme'. In either case, however simple or complex, a designer and a stand contractor are engaged to construct, install and subsequently demount the stand. Normally, separate contractors are made available for the supply of furniture, floral decoration, telephone and cleaning – although some of these items may be included as a package in the organiser's space price to the exhibitor. The stand contractor has an important responsibility in ensuring that the structure of the stand is safe and that it complies with detailed regulations supplied by the organiser as well as those imposed by a local authority or fire officer.

BUYERS

Exhibitors

The exhibitors are those companies or persons who enter a written contract with an exhibition organiser to participate in an exhibition, on the basis of an identifiable stand or area of space, in anticipation that a reasonable number of people will attend.

Participants in exhibitions are there primarily to sell goods and services, but in some instances, exhibitions are a unique opportunity to research particular markets.

Which sectors of industry and commerce are the main users of exhibitions? Figure 4.3 shows how the total number of exhibitions in 1991 divides up into the various sectors.

The discrepancy between the two pie charts – number of events and visitor numbers – is largely a function of the difference between *consumer* events (open to the general public) and *trade* (business to business) events. 'Home and lifestyle', for example, includes the Ideal Home Exhibition and 'Transport' includes the London Motor Show, both with large public attendances. By comparison, very few of the 115 'Industrial' shows are open to the general public.

Prior to making a decision to participate in an exhibition, companies usually seek information on the organiser's track record, and verify attendance figures of previous events and the extent to which these are supported by the industry sector. The organiser's contract terms, regulations and event publicity programme are also carefully studied before the final decision is taken.

Once committed, the company often appoints an executive coordinator with responsibility for overall planning, budget, stand staffing, and publicity. For a successful exhibition to be realised, exhibitors require

(a) Number of events by industry sector in 1991

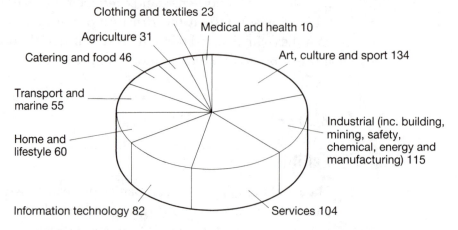

(b) Percentage of the total number of visitors who attended events in each sector

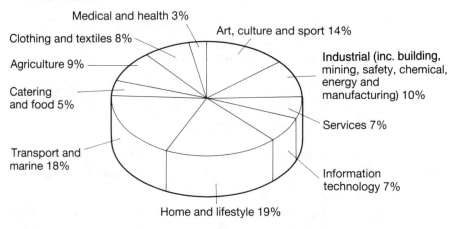

Figure 4.3   How the total number of exhibitions in 1991 divides up into various sectors
Source: Exhibition Industry Federation research

a concerted effort from several departments within the company (Personnel, Finance, Marketing, etc.).

In order to get the maximum benefit from their attendance at an exhibition, most exhibitors will undertake some form of promotional activity to draw attention to their presence at the event. They will:

● notify existing and potential customers of their participation in the event, using direct mail;

- undertake advertising in relevant publications;

- organise some activity to draw visitors to the stand – for example, demonstration of products, a competition, a celebrity, or a prize presentation.

Audience/exhibition visitors

Exhibition visitors can 'vote with their feet'. All the efforts of exhibition organisers and exhibitors will have been in vain if the visitor goes away in a disgruntled frame of mind, never to return. For that person has also 'invested' in the exhibition, whether as a trade buyer or a member of the public. The visitor's experience must be of the highest quality. Adequate provision should be made for refreshments, toilets and rest areas, as the bare minimum. Additional facilities which can be made available to visitors include post, telephone, fax, restaurants, and an efficient product information system. A simplified show guide, at a modest cost, should also be available in addition to a more elaborate and expensive version which becomes a reference book for the future.

Many exhibitions lay claim to an international status and, as such, are expected to provide an interpreter service, an overseas visitors' lounge, and multi-lingual information staff. Professional visitors, in particular, are likely to judge an exhibition by the quality and accessibility of these various services. Exhibitions are all about looking and learning, touching and trying, and the visitor approach should be tailored to that end.

The success of an exhibition can only be determined by its profitability to both types of buyer: exhibitors and visitors, each of whom has invested in the event and expects to enjoy a return. Profit for the exhibitor centres on good attendance – visitors serious in buying and stopping at their stand. The visitor will find the exhibition profitable if products are displayed which will increase turnover or offer a potential gain and if new contacts are made or a particular need is satisfied. Successful achievement of exhibitor/visitor 'profit' will bring the organiser their own reward.

THE EXHIBITION INDUSTRY FEDERATION

Launched during London's International Confex '88 exhibition, the Exhibition Industry Federation (EIF) is a trade association representing three sectors of the exhibitions industry: venue owners, exhibition organisers and contractors. The main thrust of its work lies in commissioning and publishing research and annual statistics, representing the UK exhibitions industry to the Government and the EC, and cooperating with the Department of Trade and Industry in promoting UK exhibitions to overseas visitors.

One of the EIF's principal aims is to encourage more companies to consider including exhibitions in their marketing plans, and much of the research they commission is designed to demonstrate the efficacy of this marketing technique.

It also works closely with the BTA to develop new bookings from UK and overseas events organisers and to attract more overseas visitors to trade fairs and exhibitions.

THE ASSOCIATION OF EXHIBITION ORGANISERS

For over sixty years, the Association of Exhibition Organisers (AEO) has been the focal point for firms and individuals who organise exhibitions in the UK, Europe and worldwide. Its aim is both to safeguard and promote the interests of its members and to ensure that exhibitors and all who attend shows are guaranteed the highest-quality service.

The AEO is also the place where members meet informally, through its Council and committees, seminars and discussion groups, to exchange views and information on developments, improvements and problems in the exhibition industry. The collective wealth of knowledge and experience within the AEO membership is immense.

The AEO arranges to meet ministers and officials both in the UK and in Brussels whenever there is a need to protect the interests of its members. It also keeps in close contact with the press, with the overall objective of achieving a higher share of the advertising and promotional market for exhibition organisers. The AEO is ever watchful of the effect of new legislation and regulations within the UK and the EU, and it is the coordinator when protest or lobbying is needed. It seeks to influence hall owners, contractors and all who provide services to exhibitions, in order to get the best possible terms for its members.

The AEO sponsors research and training for the benefit of its members and all those who have decided to make their career in the exhibitions industry.

The AEO's members are organisations, large and small, who can demonstrate that they have the ability and integrity to give a high standard of service to exhibitors. Members pay a membership fee calculated according to how many square metres of space the company has sold in the previous year.

BRITISH TOURIST AUTHORITY ASSISTANCE

Britain has established itself as a major country for hosting trade fairs and exhibitions. With the advent of the Single Market, more and more potential exhibitors and visitors from across the Atlantic and from other parts of the world are looking to make inroads into Europe, and the easiest initial approach is to visit or take part in a trade fair or exhibition in Britain, where most of them can use a language which is known to them – English.

Over 10 per cent of all visitors to UK exhibitions are overseas buyers, and *International Passenger Survey* statistics for 1990 showed that overseas visitors to exhibitions accounted for 7 per cent of all inward business spending in the UK.

EU residents made up 50 per cent of trade fair/exhibition visitors to Britain, with Germany (14 per cent) and France (13 per cent) the largest sources of such visitors. Nine per cent came from the USA. The second quarter of the year is usually the most popular for trade fair/exhibition visitors and London attracts well over half of this type of visit – although the Midlands, with the National Exhibition Centre, also benefits appreciably from this market.

How does the Business Travel department of the BTA promote UK exhibitions to the overseas market? For trade fair organisers, the BTA offers every year joint-scheme pump-priming funding, to enhance their overseas promotion of specific events. Assistance of this kind is offered particularly to niche market exhibitions and those events targeting new territories.

Trade Fairs in Britain is a listing of all the major trade fairs being staged in Britain which have the potential to attract overseas visitors. It is produced in association with the Exhibition Industry Federation and the Department of Trade and Industry. This calendar, which includes dates where possible for the current and following year, gives details in seven languages and is distributed worldwide through British Government overseas posts and BTA offices.

Exhibition promotion seminars

In recent years, three series of seminars have been developed by the BTA in collaboration with the Exhibition Industry Federation, with the aim of encouraging cooperation between the individual suppliers within this sector. The main aim of all these seminars is not only to make Britain's fairs and exhibitions more widely known in overseas markets, but also to facilitate the purchase of travel packages by visitors to these events.

The first series of seminars aims to bring home to the travel trade the importance of the exhibitions sector and to demonstrate the ways in which transport companies and accommodation suppliers can benefit from it – notably by undertaking special cooperative campaigns with exhibition organisers and venues, so that marketable packages can be put together. The second series takes the form of workshops, which enable exhibition organisers and the interested travel trade to talk to each other on a one-to-one basis and to start working together on exhibitions-related packages. In 1992, the BTA introduced a third series of seminars when they brought over to Britain a number of overseas tour operators, to meet and arrange business with British producers.

Finally, the BTA organises inward missions of representatives of the European business travel press. These give journalists the opportunity to visit venues and learn of the wide range of events staged, together with the supporting services and facilities available. The BTA also cooperates with the Department of Trade and Industry, with the inward missions arranged by that body.

CASE STUDY

Marketing the Ideal Home Exhibition

The Ideal Home Exhibition is the UK's best-known consumer show. This Case Study is based on an article by Kathryn Pezet, the Ideal Home Exhibition press officer, writing in *Conference & Exhibition Fact Finder* magazine.

In 1993, the Ideal Home Exhibition celebrated its 70th birthday. Having successfully overcome the challenges of the ebb and flow of the economic climate in the UK for so many years, this country's most famous consumer show was confidently facing up to the recession of the early 1990s.

In 1992, the Exhibition attracted more than 600,000 visitors and 78 per cent made a purchase, spending 47 per cent more than in 1991. An amazing achievement in financially difficult times. So what makes it happen?

The overall marketing spend for the Exhibition is £1.25 million, £750,000 of which is dedicated to advertising. The account is handled by BWB & Partners, who won the account in 1990 in a six-way competitive pitch.

BWB use a multi-media strategy which concentrates on London and the Home Counties. Television and radio advertising aim to dominate the region with a heavyweight campaign and are backed up by a poster campaign on the underground and British Rail train services. The national press was used heavily for the first time in 1992, with half-page insertions running prior to the show and in the first week. Smaller-space insertions were used after this, which, combined with specialist consumer press advertisements, supported the various four-day-long feature shows that run on each weekend of the month-long exhibition.

At the beginning of 1993, Ron White, chief executive of BWB, in an interview with Kathryn Pezet, described the challenge of enticing the consumer to the Exhibition:

> Research has shown that the majority of visitors to the show come from London and the Home Counties, and consequently our overall strategy is to ensure that no one living in that area could claim not to know that the show was taking place!

The advertising thrust is supported by in-house below-the-line activity. A comprehensive media campaign targets TV and radio and both the consumer and trade press, with the dual objective of courting consumers and exhibitors. To arouse further interest in the show, competitions for tickets and prizes are also run in the regional and consumer press.

In 1992, a promotional campaign was carried out jointly with British Rail on InterCity and Network South East routes. This used posters and leaflets to promote a £1 saving on the purchase of a joint ticket incorporating BR and tube travel and entry to the exhibition.

The show's organiser, Angex Ltd, also actively courts sponsorship, either for the show overall or for nominated areas within the exhibition. The show's 1992 overall sponsors were the Departments of the Environment and Energy, who chose the Ideal Home Exhibition to communicate the launch of their 'Helping the Earth Begins at Home' campaign.

The Ideal Home mail order catalogue was also launched in 1992 and was distributed as an insert in a selection of Sunday supplement magazines, the *Radio Times*, selective distribution areas of the *TV Times*, *Woman's Weekly*, *Woman & Home*, and some regional press. It was a success as an individual proposition and also as a vehicle for advance publicity of the exhibition, and a similar exercise was planned for the 1993 show.

Exhibitors are also encouraged to run their own individual promotional campaigns and, in 1992, British Telecom used its phonecard for promotion for the first time, advertising on the cards the details of the Ideal Home Exhibition.

Ivan Allen, the exhibition's director, sums up the publicity strategy as follows:

> We are always looking for ways to keep the exhibition in the public eye, which in turn makes it more attractive for our exhibitors. Our commitment to attracting the top names in each sector of the show as well as the gadgets and gismos that the exhibition is so famous for makes sure that the consumer keeps coming back for more.

The NOP exit survey commissioned annually by the organisers bears out this comment. Of those interviewed in 1992, 38 per cent had also visited in 1991 and 35 per cent in previous years. First-time visitors made up 27 per cent of the total and they had learnt about the exhibition chiefly from newspapers, but recommendations from friends and relatives also featured strongly as a reason, further emphasising customer loyalty to the exhibition.

The fact that 92 per cent of people rated the exhibition as enjoyable is testament to Angex's continuing success at providing a show packed with interesting and appealing features.

The past few years have seen the expansion of the exhibition into the new Earls Court 2 exhibition centre and the introduction of specialist shows, such as the highly popular 1992 Good Food Show and Fitness Expo '93, the UK's first fitness-dedicated exhibition. Such developments have succeeded in maintaining the interest of consumers and the higher-spending ABC1s, who accounted for 65 per cent of those attending in 1992.

Consumer confidence in the ability of the organisers Angex to put together good shows year after year has also recently been reflected in the trade. The Society of Motor Manufacturers and Traders who organise the Motor Show approached Angex in 1991 with the idea of staging an Ideal Home show alongside the 1992 Motor Show. The combined Autumn Ideal Home Show and the Motor Show opened to the public on 24 October 1992 and was a spectacular success. It achieved, during the nine-day period, increased visitor attendance of more than 200,000 over the figure for the 1990 Motor Show.

TRENDS

Impact of the recession

In 1991, the total amount of space hired for the 660 exhibitions recorded in major British venues amounted to 2.3 per cent less than the space used by exhibitions in 1990. But as the actual *number* of exhibitions notified in 1991 represented a 15 per cent drop (from 779 in 1990), this suggests that it was small or marginal exhibitions which did not recur in 1991.

Figure 4.4 shows the total expenditure on UK exhibitions by venue, from 1983 to 1991.

(Figures on spending on exhibitions need, however, to be viewed with caution, because of the difficulties of year-on-year comparisons in this industry. Many large exhibitions are either biennial – for example, the Motor Show – or triennial, and their appearance or non-appearance can often have a significant effect on year-on-year comparisons.)

The steep rise in spending on this sector from 1983, culminating in a spend of £562 million in 1989 can be clearly seen. The 2 per cent drop in spend on exhibitions between 1990 and 1991 compares favourably with an overall decline in all UK media spend of some 10 per cent in

	1983	1984	1985	1986	Year 1987	1988	1989	1990	1991
Earls Court & Olympia 1 & 2	30	42	42	40	38.6	37.8	39.1	32.8	35.3
NEC	27	35	35	41	37.4	39.6	38.8	42.4	36.7
Others	43	23	23	19	24	22.6	22.1	24.8	28
Total expenditure (£m)	153	191	192	258	329	495	562	549	539

(Leftmost axis label: Percentage of total expenditure)

Figure 4.4   Total expenditure on exhibitions by venue
Source: The Incorporated Society of British Advertisers, *Exhibition Expenditure Survey 1991*

1991. This indicates that exhibitions are tending to hold their market position in a general media depression.

This was confirmed in February 1993, when the EIF announced that 1992 had seen the number of exhibitions taking place in the UK grow back to the 1989 figure of over 700 events.

Independent auditing of trade shows

Estimating the overall attendances for major UK exhibitions is a complex matter because of the many uncertainties that exist. Many attendance figures are unaudited and not compiled on a regular or consistent basis, for example. (Estimating the number of overseas visitors to UK exhibitions is easier, due to the *International Passenger Survey*.) So, how do exhibitors know if a particular exhibition is worth attending? How do they know if they can expect 10 enquiries at their stand or 1,000? A new development means that it is now much easier for potential exhibitors to have access to the kind of reliable information they need to help them decide whether it is worth being represented at certain exhibitions.

In 1993, the Audit Bureau of Communications (ABC) launched an initiative to provide independently audited data on exhibition attendance. Audited exhibitions now receive a *Certificate of Attendance* and organisers are able to use the official ABC logo on exhibition correspondence. The certificate provides details of attendance, stand space occupied, number of stands and number of exhibitor personnel at the show. The audit also provides a breakdown of registered attendance according to geographical location of visitors as well as an analysis of attendance according to job title and size and type of company.

Although since 1990 all AEO members have been required to audit their exhibitions to the standard now required by the ABC, this is the first time an industry-wide standard has been established. As well as providing exhibition organisers with a statement of integrity and quality, this initiative also brings UK exhibition data up to the standards already available for shows on the Continent. This means that UK events can now be included in European directories of trade shows, which was not possible before.

Questions

1 What are the three main categories of exhibition? Give an example of each.

2 What are the principal advantages of exhibitions for (a) the exhibitors, (b) the visitors?

3 What are the advantages of combining exhibitions with related conferences?

Assignments

1 Collect as much information as you can about major exhibitions held in your country. These are often promoted in the trade and specialist press or by Chambers of Commerce. Draw up a chart listing, for each event, information under the following headings: the Exhibition Hall, the Organisers, the Stand and Service Contractors (if known), the Exhibitors, and the Audience.

2 You have been asked by the British Food Export Council Trade Association to organise a major trade fair with the aim of promoting British food to overseas markets. The event will be held in London. Draw up a plan of action, following the list of tasks normally carried out by exhibition organisers, as shown on page 101. Demonstrate how you will:

- Find suitable exhibitors
- Publicise the event
- Define the profile of the event
- Create its image
- Devise a theme
- Devise a marketing plan.

Key terms   Before moving on to the next chapter, make sure you understand the meaning of the following terms:

Consumer shows

Exhibitions organisers

Stand and service contractors

Audience

Independent auditing

5

Transport for business tourism

INTRODUCTION

Those travelling for work-related purposes use a variety of forms of transport, most of which are also used by leisure travellers. But business travellers have particular needs which make them a very distinct market for the various transport operators involved in getting them from A to B.

What special demands do business travellers make on transport operators?

Speed

People travelling on business – and those employing them – are very likely to be concerned with the speed of any transport service. While those on holiday may be content to get to their destination at a leisurely pace, with several stops along the scenic route, the business traveller is in more of a hurry. Employers are reluctant to have their highly-paid executives spending two whole working days travelling from London to Aberdeen and back by train, for example, when they can undertake the same journey in a fraction of that time by air. The reason for this concern with speed is best summed up by the British Airways advertisement with the slogan: 'Concorde leaves London at 10.30am and arrives in New York at 9.20am, *because time is money*'.

Comfort

Peace and quiet are essential elements of any transport service aimed at the business market. First of all, the business passenger may wish to use the travelling time in order to work: preparing a speech, checking figures, or reading through some notes in preparation for a meeting. Secondly, he or she may simply want to relax or even sleep in order to arrive at their destination refreshed and ready to do business effectively. In either case, the opportunity to stretch out and relax and enjoy freedom from distractions and noise is at a premium.

Reliability and punctuality

For the business traveller, the reliability and punctuality of any transport service are important considerations. Conferences and other business meetings will not normally wait for the delegate stuck in heavy traffic, sitting in a station after a cancelled train, or 35,000 feet up in the air in an aircraft which has been severely delayed. Transport operators, in their advertising aimed at this market, often emphasise their reputation for punctuality. InterCity, for example, was pleased to publish figures showing that between 1991/92 and 1992/93 the punctuality of their services (trains arriving on time or within 10 minutes) had gone up from 84 per cent to 87 per cent, while their reliability (percentage of services run) had risen from 98 per cent to 99 per cent.

Convenience

Linked with their need for speed is business travellers' demand for convenience: for transport which leaves from a convenient location and which arrives close to their final destination – at convenient times of the day. Executives want as far as possible to avoid connections, which lengthen the travel chain and increase the possibility of complications. Also, they want to leave and arrive at times which fit in conveniently with their working day. International flights from regional airports can greatly add to the convenience of air travel, as do services which get passengers to their destination at the beginning of the working day. No one wants to arrive at JFK Airport or Preston train station at 3am.

Frequency

Services which are frequent add to the efficiency factor for travelling executives. A flight route which is flown by an airline only once a day or a few times a week means that business travellers may waste time by arriving too early at their destination or by having to wait a long time for their flight home. Frequent services mean that companies' employees can get half a day's work done in the office, for example, before catching their plane or train. British Midland publicise their 8 return flights per day service between London and Brussels with the slogan: 'Heathrow – Brussels. Simply the most'.

Value for money

In times of economic stringency, value for money is an important consideration for those buying business travel. The transport operators who can offer all of the above factors at a price which is acceptable to the business market are those most likely to succeed in this highly competitive field.

AIR TRANSPORT

Classes of travel

Who gets to sit where on aircraft carrying business passengers? The choice for the passenger is usually that of luxurious first class, at the front of the plane, the much more spartan economy class at the back, or business class somewhere in between. But, in fact, when his or her company is paying for the flight, the business traveller often has no real choice: positions in the class war in the sky are often determined in advance, back on the ground. And the determining factor is usually the travelling executive's company's travel policy as discussed in Chapter 7.

Not unexpectedly, the higher the management grade, the more likely the passenger is to be allowed to travel first or business class. However, some companies, in their travel policies, do make a distinction between long-haul and short-haul flights when it comes to laying down the rules as to who is entitled to what. Figure 5.1 demonstrates the class system as it is operated by the UK companies participating in an American Express survey on business travel expenditure.

Short-haul flights

	Board directors	Senior managers	Middle and junior managers
First class	12%	2%	1%
Business class	44%	34%	18%
Economy	36%	56%	73%
Depends/varies	8%	8%	8%

Long-haul flights

	Board directors	Senior managers	Middle and junior managers
First class	23%	6%	2%
Business class	45%	45%	32%
Economy	14%	29%	41%
Depends/varies	18%	20%	25%

Figure 5.1   Class of air travel allowed for management grades
Source: *Business Travel & Expense Management Report 1992*, published by American Express Europe Ltd

Seat width and seat pitch (the amount of leg-room passengers have) are important indicators of comfort level, and of class. The more leg-room available between seats, the higher the level of luxury, as the passenger is able to stretch out in comfort during the flight. Seat pitch varies enormously, from 30 inches in some economy class cabins to the generous 55 inches available to passengers on Continental Airlines' BusinessFirst class.

In some cases, the actual seats in economy and business class are identical; what distinguishes them is not only the seat pitch, but also their 'configuration' or layout. This is the number of seats fitted abreast across the aircraft. The long-haul economy class configuration, for example, is often eight across (2–4–2), while in business class, it is more likely to be a more comfortable seven across (2–3–2).

Some airlines choose to abandon the class system completely and become, instead, one-class carriers. Examples of these are British Midland, Air UK and the Swedish independent Transwede, which all sell their seats at the lower, economy tariffs. However, the majority continue to grade their seats into different categories of comfort. Each category has its own characteristics and privileges.

First class travel

Each fare-paying first class passenger contributes highly to the airline's profitability. From September 1991 to September 1992, for example, BA's first class revenue was about £249 million. On some airlines, one first class fare between London and New York is about the equivalent of 18 stand-by specials for the same journey.

At almost £4,000 for such a trip, who actually travels first class, and why? Jenny Woolf, writing on this subject in the *Daily Telegraph* of 14 November, 1992, gives the answers:

> British Airways counts among their regular first class passengers, not only members of the royal family and their entourages, but also celebrities and rich families – the 'patricians' BA calls them – who would never dream of travelling any other way. Others travel first class on the trip of a lifetime – golden wedding couples and honeymooners, for example.

However, the typical first class passenger is travelling for business purposes. For business travellers, what are the advantages of first class air travel? These might be summed up in three words: space, comfort and exclusivity.

The privileges begin long before take-off. Private relaxing lounges and accelerated check-in facilities await first class passengers at the airport of departure. To get to the airport, many of them will have used the airport transport services which are part of the package for many airlines: for example, Air Canada offers its first class passengers a door-to-airport limousine service with car phones included.

In the air, everything possible is done to ensure the maximum comfort of first class travellers. There is no uncomfortable middle seat of three, so passengers only have one neighbour; there is no problem stretching out, no queuing for toilets or for disembarkation. First class also offers smaller cabins, seats which recline almost horizontally to afford better sleep, individual video screens and video libraries, and the best food and wine that a cramped galley can produce.

To this list, individual airlines add their own 'extras', ranging from the very practical to the extremely eccentric: for example, Virgin Atlantic has, on some flights, an in-flight beauty therapist; American Airlines has its own Professor of Oenology who chooses the wines for its first class passengers; and Royal Brunei Airlines has its first class toilets fitted with gold-plated fittings!

But first class air travel for business purposes is, in general, on the decline. This is due to two developments: improved travel conditions for business class passengers and economy measures made necessary by the financial situation of the early 1990s.

First, the new and improved business class cabins, and the associated ground facilities which most airlines introduced in the 1980s, have successfully competed with first class travel for many years now. Second, the enormous price differential (as a rule of thumb, business class costs around half the cost of a first class traveller's seat), combined with a tough economic climate, has caused many travellers to abandon first class in favour of its cheaper alternative.

Consequently, many airlines have been reducing the size of their first class cabins, or abolishing them altogether. For example, Singapore Airlines, Swissair, Lufthansa and Cathay Pacific have reconfigured their first class compartments to make more room for business class seats. Cathay virtually halved the number of first class seats in its 747-200s, and its new Boeing 777s have no first class compartments on board, only economy and business class.

As Gillian Upton wrote in an article on this subject in the March 1993 edition of *Business Traveller* magazine:

> Corporate insistence that company executives downtrade is continuing apace, and will keep first class cabins relatively empty for the foreseeable future. Consider that a company executive who flies to New York ten times a year in business class instead of first can save his/her company a massive £17,840. Multiply that by the number of executives doing the same trip and the wisdom of downtrading is very evident.

While first class travel within Europe has now disappeared, the highly competitive transatlantic routes still comprise the biggest first class market. But how many passengers in those seats have actually paid the full first class fare? Many passengers have been upgraded into first: because business class has been overbooked, because the airline wants to hang on to regular customers in a competitive environment, or because a traveller has earned a seat there through his/her frequent flyer scheme. One of the reasons Continental Airlines gave for abolishing first class altogether a few years ago was that only 5 per cent of first class passengers were revenue generating. British Airways claims that 'the majority' of its first class passengers have paid for their tickets.

Business class

Business class seats are to be found in a separate compartment that falls half-way between the luxuries of first and the economies of economy class. Many airlines use their own terminology for this class: Club World (British Airways), Euroclass (SAS) and Raffles (Singapore Airlines).

These seats cost at least three or four times the economy class fare. Is it worth it? There is no doubt that it is worth it for the airlines. A Jumbo jet flying from London to New York with nobody in either economy or first class would still make a profit if business class were full.

But, for the passenger, what are the benefits of travelling business class? How do the airlines seek to justify the great differential between business and economy class fares?

Incentives designed to woo business class passengers fall into two categories: on the ground and in the air. Pre-take-off perks can begin at the traveller's own front door, as chauffeur-driven limousine transfers to the airport are increasingly used to pamper passengers. For example, Cathay Pacific is one of a growing number of airlines offering limousine transfers or free airport parking to their business class passengers. Once at the airport, the business class passenger is more than likely to spend some time in an exclusive lounge which combines armchair comfort with business facilities. British Airways leads the airlines in its provision of lounge facilities. To its already impressive range of lounges at Heathrow – Clubworld, Speedbird for 'CIPs' (Commercially Important People) and the Oasis lounge with showers – it added in 1992 what it claims is the largest business class lounge in Europe, complete with 40 telephones, fax machines and photocopiers, and space for up to 400 passengers.

In the air, the airlines are coming up with ever more ingenious ways of justifying business class. In addition to having better food and more comfortable seats than those travelling in economy, as well as individual armrest television sets offering a personal choice of entertainment, business class passengers increasingly have access to a wide range of services made possible through sophisticated in-flight technology. On the leisure side, in-flight shopping by mail order, the booking of theatre seats or hotel rooms, or playing electronic games are all possible, thanks to the new on-board computers being installed by airlines.

But the same technology can be put to a quite different use. It can offer on-board telephones, fax and computer links, providing virtual 'offices in the sky' for industrious business class passengers.

On the face of it, flying offices make good sense for both airlines and their business passengers, as Renate Lederer, a Munich travel expert, recently wrote:

> In an era of corporate cost-cutting, airlines are under pressure to justify the considerable price differential between business and economy class. Flying offices provide airlines with a way to link greater productivity on the part of the individual business traveller.

But, as airlines struggle to keep up with each other by installing more and more sophisticated entertainment and office facilities, the question is also being asked: how many business class passengers really need to use, for example, satellite-based telecommunication relays and air-to-ground teleconferencing? The reply of many travellers themselves is that, apart from the peace and quiet needed in order to rest a little or go through a few documents, all most business class passengers want is some light entertainment and relaxation. In a *Business Traveller* magazine straw poll of readers in February 1993, opinions on the subject of the benefits of in-flight technology were divided:

> The plane is the only place I can get a bit of peace and quiet. I really enjoy getting on a flight and knowing I can't be disturbed for ten hours. (L. Phipps)

> I find it very useful to know I can be contacted, but the opportunity to book hotel rooms would not affect my choice of airline. I like the idea of more in-flight entertainment and would definitely choose an airline with this facility in preference to one without it. (P. Sutch)

> I like to think I'm organised enough with my travel arrangements not to have to worry about booking hotel rooms. I like the idea of better in-flight entertainment and can't wait until it's more readily available. (P. Tucker)

Phone service

IMAGINE a hectic round of overseas meetings, a rush to the airport, and a long wait in the departure lounge. You finally sink into your seat for the long flight back and a bit of rest – just as the passenger beside you picks up the phone for an argument with his wife, and a child on the other side settles down to play the latest video game with a steady click, click, click on the keypad.

Welcome to the new world of air travel, courtesy of Mercury, which, with American and Irish partners, wants to put a phone into the armrest of every aircraft seat. The service will enable a passenger to bring his office with him – plug in his laptop computer, send faxes, make airline, entertainment and hotel bookings, check stock market prices and so on. If bored, he can use the handset buttons to play computer games on a screen fixed to the chair in front.

The phone side works like a giant digital cellular network, with base stations on the ground or satellites in space picking up calls and feeding them into traditional phone networks.

All Mercury and its partners need are airlines prepared to have their aircraft kitted out with the hardware and enough passengers to use and pay for the service. Perhaps what most passengers will need is the chance, when checking in, to get away from it all.

"Phoning or non-phoning, sir?"

Figure 5.2
Source: *The Guardian*, 7 July, 1993

Will demand be sufficiently high to justify the massive investment in in-flight technology for passengers? Time will tell. But in the meantime, as the costly equipping of offices at 30,000 feet up goes on, the anxiety felt by some passengers is expressed in the extract from an article by Alex Brummer in *The Guardian* given in Figure 5.2.

Economy class

Many of the strenuous attempts by airlines to woo business class passengers have been made necessary by the growing uptake of economy seats by business travellers – despite the restrictions imposed on a great deal of economy class travel, inability to make last-minute changes to travel arrangements being the most widespread.

Many airlines have responded by creating 'full economy' class sections in their economy class cabins. These provide full-fare-paying passengers (typically business travellers, who need the flexibility of a full-fare

Why fares are just pie in the sky

BUSINESS people all across Europe may grumble about the cost of the continent's air fares, but nowadays the price of an airline ticket is determined largely by market forces. The greater variety of competition on routes to and from the UK enables British business travellers to come off best, but their counterparts elsewhere in Europe are having to pay through the nose, despite the open market.

Practically every route in Europe outside Britain is controlled by two airlines at most, both charging identical fares.

This means that the German banker flying from Frankfurt to Brussels ($485 return: 90 cents per km) pays 25 per cent more for a flexible ticket – one allowing flight changes without penalty – than does his or her counterpart flying from London to Brussels ($387 return: 64 cents per km).

The price discrepancy is even greater in the case of a Parisian booking a flexible ticket to Stockholm. He or she pays up to a staggering 75 per cent more than the Londoner flying to Stockholm.

The latter pays a top business class fare of $735 return (29 cents per km) to fly from Heathrow with British Airways or SAS, Scandinavian Airlines. Or the Londoner can pay as little as $375 return (15 cents per km) for a flexible economy class ticket with City Air Scandinavia from London City Airport.

The Parisian, on the other hand, has no choice of fare at all. His or her cheapest ticket would be business class from Paris with Air France or SAS at the whopping price of Ffr 8,040 ($1,450): 55 cents per km

Alex McWhirter on wide disparities in the cost of European flights

– nearly four times more than the Londoner pays.

Business people who have no choice but to patronise thinly used monopolistic routes lose out even more. At 175 cents per km, the 332 km round-trip Geneva-Turin service (flown solely by the Swissair subsidiary Crossair) costing Sfr756 ($504) must surely be Europe's most expensive international flight, based on cost per km.

Likewise, it comes as no surprise to learn that on this basis Air UK's monopoly Norwich-Amsterdam service (480 km round-trip) is the UK's costliest international fare at $414: 97 cents per kilometre.

Fares can also be distorted over the years by government action. When SAS was asked why its Paris-Stockholm business class fare was so much higher than the London-Stockholm one, a spokesman replied: "Fares from France are higher than those from the UK because the UK CAA [Civil Aviation Authority] has pursued a different policy from its French counterpart.

"The UK CAA has been reluctant to approve any fare increases, including those in line with inflation, so UK-Scandinavia business fares remained unchanged between 1984 and 1989. During the same period, the French authorities approved most fare increases filed by the airlines."

Surely business people can cut costs by down-grading to economy class? They can in the case

of flights to and from Britain, where either flexible economy and/or less flexible Eurobudget tariffs are available.

But this option is not readily available for business travellers within mainland Europe, where it is usually a case of business class or nothing at all. What economy fares are on offer tend to be very restrictive and require executives to spend a Saturday night away from home – which is not, of course, an acceptable business option.

Two airlines, SAS and Swissair, recently brought in fares lower than business class (provided passengers meet a few restrictions), aimed at business travellers flying from Scandinavia or from Switzerland. But the situation involving flights from and between France, Germany and Italy remains bleak.

In the long run, the experience with deregulation in the United States does not bode well for the European business person, for it reveals that leisure travellers (who can meet booking restrictions) have benefited at the expense of their business traveller counterparts.

Figures released by the US National Economic Research Association show that between 1977 and 1991 the average cost of US domestic flights rose by 49 per cent, yet, during the same period, the average price of flexible fares rose by 262 per cent.

Clearly, the airlines have exploited business travellers' need for flexible travel arrangements, and there is no easy answer. Because, as was pointed out in the first place, air fares are now dictated by the market place.

Figure 5.3
Source: *The European*, 1–4 April, 1993

ticket) with a range of added benefits, such as more spacious seats, free drinks and a choice of meals.

One example of this is the Japanese carrier All Nippon Airways, which in 1992 introduced a fourth class for full-fare economy passengers. This Comfort Plus class caters for only six passengers and is contained within the normal economy class cabin. But seats in this class offer four more inches than the normal 34-inch economy pitch and also feature leg rests.

However, if trading down to economy class is a viable option for British businesses, for their continental counterparts it is usually a case of business class or nothing at all, as shown in the article in Figure 5.3, which draws attention to the wide disparities in the cost of European business travel by air.

CASE
STUDY

Virgin Atlantic and Jane

Top of the bill in Virgin's host of enticements for the business class passenger is Jane, the personal masseuse of both Richard Branson and his wife, now turned in-flight healer and regularly to be found caressing the scalps of executives as they descend into New York. Kneading of shoulders and manicuring of hands are other features of her services, along with aromatherapy, mouthwashes and other jet lag antidotes, all designed to help travellers arrive at their destinations feeling perky and wide awake.

En route, seated in the 2–2 configuration, passengers have meals on fine bone china, films on television screens that pop out of the armrests and free gifts ranging from compact discs and pens to torches and comfort kits. On arrival, they are offered a helicopter ride into New York or a shuttle boat into Boston, depending on the destination.

On top of all the added-value services, the airline throws in Freeway Rewards, a sophisticated air miles system for frequent travellers. In association with Budget-Rent-a-Car, Holiday Inn and Visa, it offers not only free trips, but also the opportunity to sample a variety of exclusive leisure activities including health club stays, polo at Ascot, ballooning, hang-gliding, a photo safari in Kenya and trips on the Orient Express.

In 1992, Virgin introduced a new 'Mid Class' service on its flights. This gives full-fare-paying passengers in economy the equivalent of a business class-sized seat on any other airline. Mid Class passengers have their own separate check-in counters and priority baggage handling (although the food is the same as that in economy class). The biggest advantage of Mid Class, from the point of view of the company paying for the ticket, is that the price is only a third of the £2,000 cost of a business class return from London to New York on other airlines. (Virgin's Upper Class seats – which sell at business class prices – are the equivalent of first class seats on other airlines.)

The differences between Virgin's Upper and Mid Class seats and their equivalents with other airlines is shown in Figure 5.4.

Figure 5.4 Virgin Atlantic advertisement
Source: Courtesy of Virgin Atlantic Airways

Frequent flyer schemes

Until the arrival of the big US airlines in Europe, European airlines were happy simply to offer their business passengers enhanced service to keep them coming back. That is no longer enough, now that passengers have felt the lure of free travel generated by mileage-based frequent flyer schemes.

These schemes are a brand loyalty-inducing idea: by flying with the same airline, passengers are able to accumulate 'miles' or 'points' which give them access to a range of perks. Points may also be accumulated by travellers patronising other suppliers such as hotels or car rental firms. The perks on offer through these schemes include not only free airline tickets, but also upgrade privileges, additional excess baggage allowances, expedited check-in, admission to airport lounges, and the guarantee of a seat even when flights are fully booked to 'normal' passengers.

Due to the immense popularity of these schemes, airlines throughout the world have been obliged to imitate the US airlines by introducing their own schemes, in order to compete for passengers.

As Mike Swindell and Mike Ager reported in the 23 July, 1992 edition of *TTG Europa*, British Airways was the first into the European market with a full-blown frequent flyer programme based on its Air Miles and Latitudes schemes. Alitalia was also quick off the mark with its Club Ulisse programme, which also gives free tickets as well as a range of service enhancements. In May 1992, Iberia joined in, with a scheme called Iberia Plus. Free tickets can be used by Iberia Plus cardholders, their family or travelling companions.

At the beginning of June 1992, KLM extended its Flying Dutchman frequent flyer programme from the Dutch market to the rest of Europe. Its mileage points can now be earned from flights on Air UK, KLM Cityhopper and North West Airlines. This programme offers a range of benefits that includes unusual deals such as cordon bleu cookery sessions, yachting and skiing, as well as free travel.

Air France joined in rather late, with Frequence Plus, which it launched for French passengers in June 1992, with the intention of introducing it progressively throughout its European markets. By March 1993, British residents had been accepted into the scheme. Points earned on the scheme can be redeemed for free flights (eight London–Paris round trips earn sufficient points for a free London–Nice ticket), upgrades and excess baggage allowances.

The trend towards frequent flyer programmes has now also spread to Asian and Far Eastern airlines, which for years were able to command loyalty from passengers simply on the strength of their outstanding passenger service. They have now begun introducing frequent flyer programmes, in response to the competition created by US carriers aggressively promoting their loyalty schemes. Japan Airlines launched a mileage bank in January 1993, allowing passengers from Europe, the Middle East and Africa to redeem points for flight class upgrades, hotel accommodation, holiday vouchers and free tickets to Japan and beyond. In summer 1993, Singapore Airlines, Cathay Pacific and Malaysia Airlines launched their own frequent flyer programmes.

From the business traveller's point of view, are the perks offered by airline frequent flyer schemes sufficiently attractive to bind them to one airline? *Business Traveller* magazine carried out a straw poll of its readers in the March 1993 issue, and the responses to the above question make interesting reading:

> W. Lessar thinks they are fine for people who make regular journeys to the same country, but he wouldn't touch them personally. 'I have got to the age when I can treat myself to business class so I enjoy many perks there. I prefer to check out the various deals available and choose the one with the best offer. It might be an idea for the airlines to offer something completely different as an incentive, such as a cruise.'

> W. Jaspert is a big fan of the US flyer schemes which have had plenty of time to get things right. 'The main disadvantages of the European schemes are their lack of interchangeability and the few facilities where mileage credit can be used.'

> R. Kleiner points out the drawbacks: 'The perks in real terms are not all that great, especially for regular short-haul travellers. Schemes should differentiate between short- and long-haul travellers. Someone making two long-haul flights a year would accumulate more points than someone like me travelling short-haul every week.'

Nevertheless, there is growing evidence that these schemes play a vital role in determining customers' choice of airline. An American Express Business Barometer survey in 1992 claimed that 75 per cent of the companies contacted reported that frequent flyer programmes for regular travellers *did* affect their purchasing decisions; and a Lifestyle survey conducted at the same time by *Official Airline Guides* revealed that first and business class passengers rate an airline's frequent flyer programme almost as high as punctuality and on-board comfort. It is for this reason that every quality airline in Europe now has to offer a frequent flyer scheme. If it doesn't, its best customers will simply defect to the competition who do.

Another question which needs to be answered is this: should the benefits earned through frequent flyer schemes go to the company (which, after all, pays for the ticket) or to the individual traveller?

In a MORI telephone research poll conducted among 300 travel bookers and 100 decision makers in September 1992, on behalf of Wagon-lits Travel UK, opinion was divided on this issue. However, 57 per cent of companies interviewed believed that travellers should *not* personally be the recipients of the perks offered by the airlines. The research report quoted two decision makers as follows:

> In every other procurement activity, if there is a discount being offered, it will come back to the company. I don't see why the individual should get it.

> Companies really and truly want to do something to stop it. The benefits really should come back to the company.

This criticism of the schemes themselves was not, however, extended to the business travel agencies used by companies to buy their flights. Only 7 per cent of those interviewed believed that business travel agencies promoted airlines offering frequent flyer schemes rather than airlines offering the best deal.

TRENDS

During the 1970s and 1980s, average annual growth worldwide in air travel was in the region of 8 per cent. But by the early 1990s, this sector was facing serious problems. Air transport is a sector which is extremely sensitive to the business cycle: it tends to be one of the first sectors to be affected by an economic downturn. And the economics of airline operation are such that even quite a small reduction in average seat factors (the proportion of seats actually occupied by fare-paying passengers) can make the difference between profit and loss.

Given this, it is hardly surprising that the early 1990s were disastrous for the world's airlines. Due mainly to the economic downturn, most airlines experienced substantial losses. On the basis of Revenue Passenger Kilometres, world airline output declined by 4 per cent in 1991, the first fall since reliable records began in the 1940s.

But not all airlines suffered to the same extent. Buoyant economies generate high levels of demand for air transport, and the booming economies of the Asia/Pacific region ensured that airlines based there continued to do much better than, say, their European counterparts. For example, in 1991, Malaysia Airlines actually experienced a 19 per cent *rise* in business.

Britain, with its far from buoyant economy, experienced a more severe decline in air travel than most other industrialised countries. In 1992, Barry Humphreys, Head of Air Services Policy and Industry Affairs at the UK Civil Aviation Authority, described the UK situation as follows:

> The number of passengers carried to, from and within the UK fell by 6.5 per cent in 1991 to 98.5 million. This is only the third absolute decline in the past 25 years. (Traffic fell by 7.4 per cent in 1974 and by 0.1 per cent in 1981 – both periods marked by crises, of course.) It is interesting that charter traffic seems to have held up significantly better than scheduled traffic. In Western Europe, which accounts for the bulk of charter passengers, charter demand fell by 2.1 per cent compared with an 8.5 per cent decline for scheduled services.

(This difference can be easily explained. Scheduled services were affected more by the economic downturn than their charter counterparts, as companies cut back significantly on business travel in order to save money. This directly affected demand for scheduled services; but demand for the annual Mediterranean holiday, no longer regarded as a luxury – at least for those still in employment – continued.)

However, on the positive side, the thriving economy of southern China was providing opportunities for UK companies to do business, and this benefited airlines such as Cathay Pacific. As well as increasing the frequency of its flights to that region, Cathay Pacific also expanded routes to the South-East Asian region.

By the early 1990s, most airlines were having difficulty attracting passengers into their first and business class cabins. It was a clear case of too much capacity chasing too little demand. This was a problem dating back to 1991, when airlines around the world added on average 30 per cent more seats on the strength of steady demand. When deepening recession put paid to business travel growth, airlines were left with an overcapacity.

But airlines have a built-in resistance to cut-backs on services, even in a recession. They regard this as a retrograde step and fear that cutting frequency might be seen by the public, and by the competition, as exposing weakness. Instead, then, most airlines opted for a round of price-cutting, across all classes of travel.

As a result, by the mid-1990s, airline business travellers had never had it so good. Loyalty incentives and comfort aboard aircraft were reaching new heights, and, with discounting rife in most markets, the price was right – even in the previously untouchable first and business classes, for those still able to afford these.

. . . .

CASE STUDY

London Gatwick airport and British Airways

For many business travellers, the nearest they ever get to London Gatwick airport is when they drive past the Gatwick turn-off on the M25 or M23, heading for a flight taking off from Heathrow. But what they do not realise is that, very often, there are regular flights to the same destinations leaving from Gatwick itself. In most cases, the same business travellers, and those making the flight bookings on their behalf, would be surprised to hear that Gatwick is connected to a wide and busy network which includes a vast and growing number of vital business routes. They would be even more surprised to hear of BA's and Gatwick's plans for the airport's future.

The key participant in the present and future development of London Gatwick is British Airways.

February 1993 saw the opening of a new chapter in the development of BA's services at Gatwick. The company moved 10 former Dan-Air European services from Gatwick's South Terminal to the North. To the casual observer, this might have seemed to have been a fairly routine piece of tidying up in the wake of BA's takeover of Dan-Air the previous year. In reality, it was a key piece in BA's strategy to turn its London Gatwick base into one of the world's major international hubs.

The 10 routes inherited from Dan-Air were combined with the 12 other European routes that BA had been operating out of London Gatwick for some time. The beefed-up network now includes important business routes such as Athens, Brussels, Paris, Rome and Zurich, which had been missing from the BA portfolio until the Dan-Air deal.

Now all the European routes are bound together in London Gatwick's North Terminal, together with BA's 25-route long-haul network. The fact that both long-haul and short-haul networks are operating from the same terminal is the base-block of BA's strategy to build a US-style 'hub and spoke' operation, now that all the necessary elements have come together.

The success of BA's hub and spoke operation depends on its ability to connect, with the maximum efficiency, feeder flights to and from the UK and continental Europe on to its long-haul services. Of equal importance is the exercise of getting the message across to the public at large.

On the first count, the airline has already made a good start with the re-scheduling of key North Atlantic services to Houston, Atlanta, Dallas/Fort Worth and New York so that they leave London Gatwick between 09.55 and 10.30, among the earliest transatlantic departure times in the UK. In the case of New York, the BA flight from London Gatwick is the first of the airline's JFK services of the day.

These departures are now linked into arriving flights from continental Europe. The impact of this coordination was described by Dan Brewin, BA's Senior General Manager at Gatwick:

> In some cases, we offer some of the fastest connections anywhere in Europe. By connecting through London Gatwick, a passenger can arrive in New York earlier than if he went from his own European gateway.

Getting the message across has been more of a challenge.

Research by both BA and Gatwick Airport Ltd uncovered a misconception about the airport in the minds of the travelling public and the travel trade alike. The popular misconception was that London Gatwick could not provide the range of services or frequency to satisfy the demands of business travellers for the flexibility needed by them in their arrangements.

The shift of some airlines from London Gatwick following the opening up of Heathrow to all airlines in the early 1990s, combined with the collapse of Air Europe and the failure of Dan-Air, also left many travellers – and some in the travel trade – uncertain of exactly what services London Gatwick provided.

Yet a bare catalogue of facts about London Gatwick should convince anyone that the airport is among the best in the business:

- It has a fast and efficient rail link every 15 minutes to the West End of London in the form of the Gatwick Express.

- A frequent rail service with Thameslink offers half hourly services into the City of London and to the north.

- It is adjacent to the M23 motorway, linking into the M25 and the national motorway network.

- Nearly 50 scheduled airlines, including the powerful BA, offer services to almost 130 short-haul and intercontinental destinations.

- It boasts one of the most modern terminals in the UK.

- Passengers can check in at Victoria railway station and leave their luggage to be transferred to the airport.

- There are two top-class hotels, linked to the airport by covered way, that offer convenient on-site accommodation.

To tackle this problem and to change attitudes towards the airport, Gatwick Airport Ltd and BA began working closely in a campaign of product improvement and promotion to raise the profile of the airport and exploit its potential to the full.

Product improvement

More than £40 million has been spent on upgrading facilities at Gatwick:

- A major project which started in January 1993 was the redevelopment of the North Terminal International departure lounge, to create more space and a wider choice of shops and restaurants, at a cost of £12 million.

- Nearby, the airport also began the construction of a £3 million self-contained pavilion for first and business class passengers, for completion by Spring 1994. The pavilion will house airline executive suites and duty-free shopping facilities.

- The South Terminal check-in space will also be expanded to give a feel more akin to the spacious facilities enjoyed at the newer North Terminal.

- More shopping outlets in both terminals are planned, to fall in line with the current thinking that duty-free and other shopping, including food outlets, should be conducted on a smaller scale, instead of in supermarket-style emporia.

Promotional campaign

The following measures were taken to educate the business travel market:

- Beginning early 1993, every quarter, the airport sent out 150,000 copies of a timetable combined with a free business traveller's handbook, entitled *London Gatwick Direct*, which detailed all the services available at the airport.

- A newsletter called *Directions* was distributed to the same market, to update the frequent flyer on new services.

- BA ran its own television advertising campaign, the first ever to focus specifically on London Gatwick. Promoting the carrier's drive to set up a hub-and-spoke operation at the airport, the essence of the message to potential passengers was: 'London Gatwick – the Hub without the Hubbub'.

- Gatwick ran a series of educationals for travel decision makers, from secretaries to corporate travel managers, from Europe, to demonstrate to them the range of facilities at Gatwick.

Among the most imaginative innovations at the airport was the launch in 1992 of *Fast Track*, a red carpet route through the airport for business travellers. The aim was to speed business flyers through potential bottlenecks and help them reach their destinations faster and more efficiently than through any other UK airport. Anyone with a business class or first class ticket can become a Fast Track pass holder.

The Fast Track concept starts with InterCity's London Gatwick Express service from Victoria station direct to the airport in 30 minutes. Trains run every quarter hour through the day. On arrival at London Gatwick's terminals, Fast Track becomes a dedicated rapid clearance system guiding pass holders through the usual handling processes. There is priority check-in, a priority security channel, priority passport control and a priority Fast Track through Duty Free. Fast Track pass holders can also save time picking up pre-ordered foreign currency at London Gatwick's bureaux de change. Currency can be ordered in advance so that the money is waiting at any of the dedicated Fast Track counters in the airport.

Figure 5.5   Aerial photograph of London Gatwick Airport
Source: Gatwick Airport Ltd

BA's presence at Gatwick offers the airport great opportunities for the future. It has a strong route network in both short-haul and long-haul routes, and is a worldwide airline with considerable marketing and sales strength. Together, using the above measures, the airline and the airport are seeking to lay to rest the misconceptions which dogged Gatwick's development during the 1980s and turn it into one of Western Europe's most important aerial junctions. Figure 5.5 shows an aerial view of Gatwick Airport.

(Some of the material used in this Case Study is reproduced by kind permission of BAA/Gatwick Airport Ltd.)

TRAIN TRAVEL

Rail travel offers many advantages to the business tourist. No time-consuming treks to the airport and long check-in times; no stress or wasted time sitting in heavy traffic. Instead, space, convenience, the opportunity to work, eat or simply relax in comfort, or, on night trains, the possibility of a good night's sleep in an individual bedroom.

InterCity is a self-contained business within British Rail. Its purpose is to provide a national network of fast and frequent trains linking all the major business centres in Britain. Each weekday, 780 InterCity trains run, with departure and arrival times scheduled to suit business travellers, and with a range of services designed to suit their business needs.

InterCity's main selling point for the business customer is what it calls 'usable time'. In other words, travel by InterCity trains can be used productively, by working during the journey. The stress-free nature of train travel is also emphasised as another core benefit, with passengers arriving at their destination refreshed and ready to do business. In its advertising, InterCity underlines these aspects, and makes the contrast with other forms of travel, in particular, motorway driving ('tiring and stressful') and air travel (involving 'stop-start journeys to and from out-of-town airports'). Figure 5.6 shows some examples of InterCity's advertising, from a 1993 press campaign aimed at the business community.

Classes of train travel

First class

First class compartments provide a quiet, secluded environment for uninterrupted working or rest, with attentive service, and at-seat refreshments and meals. The services available to passengers purchasing first class travel include: complimentary seat reservations, tables which provide ample working space, access to card phones, and restaurant service (on over 240 trains each weekday).

The *First Class Executive Ticket* is described by InterCity as a 'flexible package tailored to the business traveller's needs'. This all-inclusive package incorporates all the benefits of first class travel (and more) in a single booking which can be adapted to meet the passenger's individual needs. It offers the following elements:

● first class return tickets with seat reservations;

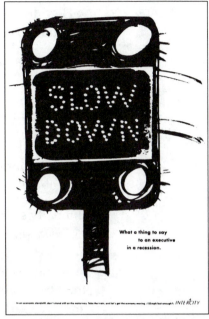

NOT ONE OF THESE PEOPLE CAN READ OR WRITE. Or study a report. Or tuck into a sandwich. Or chew over some figures. When you work it out, you'll find the train's the right choice.

SLOW DOWN. WHAT A THING TO SAY TO AN EXECUTIVE IN A RECESSION. In an economic standstill, the last thing you need is to stand still on the motorway. Take the train, and let's get the economy moving. (125 mph sound fast enough?)

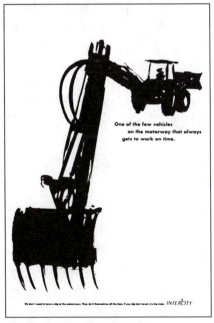

ONE OF THE FEW VEHICLES ON THE MOTORWAY THAT ALWAYS GETS TO WORK ON TIME. We don't need to have a dig at the motorways. They do it themselves almost every day of the year. If you dig fast travel, try the train.

PRACTISE YOUR MOTORWAY DRIVING. STARE INTENTLY AT THIS PAGE. Fog, ice, warning signs, hold ups. If it wasn't for the train, we'd all go dotty.

Figure 5.6   InterCity advertisements
Source: InterCity – British Rail

- London Underground Zone One return tickets (for travel to or via London);

- refreshment vouchers with ability to pre-purchase meal or sleeper options;

- free car parking;

- specially priced packages from Scotland include sleeper and/or meal options, and packages from the north-east include meal options.

InterCity's 'premier service for top business travellers', *First Class Pullman* service, is available on over 40 trains each weekday at no additional cost. First Class Pullman services use the most up-to-date air-conditioned coaches and provide the fastest and most convenient train travel between the major commercial centres of England, Scotland and Wales. Passengers on these services are entitled to: personal attention from special Pullman staff, complimentary tea and coffee served at the passenger's seat, enhanced menus with a wide range of fine wines, and an at-seat trolley service, which allows uninterrupted working.

First Class Pullman Lounges, which may be used by all first class ticket holders, are luxury waiting areas situated in certain stations: Edinburgh, London King's Cross, London Euston, Leeds and Newcastle. These are equipped with telephones, televisions with teletext, photocopiers, desks, and fax machines. Complimentary tea and coffee is served and a lounge menu is available. Meeting rooms for use of up to 10 people can also be booked at the Edinburgh, Leeds and Newcastle lounges.

Silver Standard

Silver Standard is the name given to the enhanced service for full-fare standard single and return ticket holders on selected InterCity trains. This provides separate accommodation for such passengers, complimentary tea and coffee, an at-seat refreshment service, and complimentary seat reservations.

Sleeper services

Although taking an overnight train provides a cost-effective and reliable form of travel, sleeper services have had to struggle to maintain their share of the business travel market, in the UK as well as in continental Europe. Fierce domestic airline competition has considerably reduced InterCity's Anglo-Scottish sleeper train business, as air travel allows executives to get to their destination and back on the same day – a great advantage over spending a night away from home sleeping on a train. Another problem with UK domestic sleeper services is that, because of the relatively short distances, the trains depart and arrive at anti-social hours. As the travel writer Alex McWhirter put it in a *Business Traveller* magazine article on this topic, who wants to hang around London's Euston station for a 23.35 train for Edinburgh, and what work can you do when you pull into Edinburgh at 06.00?

Despite these problems, sleeper services offer some important advantages. Price is one: the cost of taking night trains (including the first class rail fare and a single compartment) is still far less than the business class air fare. Other night train benefits include the saving on hotel bills, more reliable timekeeping in bad weather and probably a less stressful travel experience.

Accommodation standards have improved over the years. Air-conditioned cabins now feature hot and cold running water, bedside lights, temperature control and shaving points. An early morning call is accompanied by a complimentary light breakfast, tea or coffee and a morning newspaper every weekday.

Choosing the first class option when travelling by InterCity sleeper has several advantages, not the least of which is entry to the Pullman Lounge at Euston station, a welcome refuge from the crowded concourse below. The lounge, which is open from 07.00 to 23.00, is equipped with TV, telephones, fax machine and photocopier, while attentive staff offer free tea or coffee or a range of drinks and snacks.

Trends

High-speed trains

High-speed rail services around the world are giving an impetus to business travellers to move from air travel to trains, over distances where the total journey time is less than 3 hours. The early evidence surrounding the impact of high-speed trains is largely positive. The

TGV Sud-Est and TGV Atlantique in France, the ICE in Germany, Britain's IC225 between London and Edinburgh, Italy's ETR 450 first class only business trains which link Rome with the major Italian business centres, the Spanish TAV between Madrid and Seville, and Sweden's X2000 tilting train between Stockholm and Gothenburg, are all providing competitive alternatives to domestic air travel.

But the growth of high-speed train links extends beyond the boundaries of Europe. When, in Spring 1993, the train travelling time between Tokyo and Osaka, Japan's second city, was cut by 30 minutes, many commuting business travellers began swapping the plane for the train because it was quicker. The Nozomi bullet train takes 150 minutes, longer than the flying time of 60 minutes, but the saving comes on the ground. For those making the journey by air, there is an efficient 20-minute monorail journey from Tokyo to the airport; but the delays come at the other end, when trying to get from Osaka airport into the city centre. Buses and cars are the only options, and there is appalling traffic to negotiate.

Japan Airlines had to respond by cancelling one of its seven daily flights from Tokyo to Osaka because of the added competition caused by an increase in frequency to 17 daily departures of the Nozomi bullet train. The rapid increase in popularity of the bullet train came despite its fares, which in 1993 were higher than the air fare on the same route: a return bullet train ticket cost ¥30,000 (£173) compared with JAL's economy class return ticket price of ¥28,352 (£156).

Even in the US, where the airlines have long dominated inter-city travel, plans for new high-speed rail links are being drawn up. If federal funding for the project is forthcoming, Amtrak will run high-speed trains between Boston and New York. The journey, which currently takes 4½–5 hours, could be trimmed back to 3 hours if the plan to straighten out and update the existing track and undertake signal improvements gets the go-ahead. Amtrak say that the high-speed rail link could be operational by the late 1990s, and if successful, would be followed by others on important business travel routes such as San Francisco–Los Angeles, Los Angeles–San Diego and Chicago–Detroit.

But, to return to Europe, with its dense concentration of relatively small countries, one problem with the development of high-speed train links for business travel is becoming increasingly evident. As was pointed out by Mike Knutton in the January 1992 edition of *Business Traveller* magazine, while the world of business and commerce does not recognise national boundaries, none of the existing batch of European high-speed trains crosses international borders (with the exception of certain French TGV trains which operate into Switzerland). This effectively puts a serious brake on international business train travel. Mike Knutton writes:

> It is in the technical, operating and marketing aspects of intra-European railway services that future problems may lie. The technical problems of different types of electrification, different signalling systems, and different infrastructures including loading gauges and platform heights can be, and are being solved – at a price. The real problem lies in the conservative and nationalistic culture of railways, and indeed manufacturers, and their personnel. This will have to give way to higher levels of cooperation and a more customer-oriented approach based on a new 'think Europe' attitude.

If the earlier introduction of EuroCity rail services is anything to go by, then European business travellers can afford to be optimistic over the prospect of future international high-speed train services. Top-of-the-range locomotive-hauled EuroCity trains running along major European business routes, such as Paris–Amsterdam, have been highly successful. Passenger numbers are growing and new services are being introduced, some of the latest into Eastern Europe between Vienna and Budapest and Vienna and Prague. The secret of EuroCity's success lies in the very strict rules under which the services operate. For example, railways operating under the EuroCity banner must use their latest, air-conditioned coaches, and trains must offer catering, ideally a restaurant car. On-board staff have to be able to speak several languages, and, most importantly, the trains must operate at an average speed of about 100km/h.

If the same spirit of international cooperation can be applied to the development of an international high-speed train network in Europe, then business travellers will have every reason to be optimistic over the possibilities offered by this latest innovation in rail travel. The signs are good. Current plans being promoted by the Community of European Railways and the International Union of Railways look forward to a European high-speed network of more than 30,000 km by early next century, consisting of about 10,000 km of new lines, 10,000 km of upgraded lines, and 11,000 km of link and feeder lines.

The Channel Tunnel

The completion of the Channel Tunnel heralds a new era of fast train journey times to international destinations. Eurostar is the brand name for the direct, high-speed passenger rail services between Britain, France and Belgium. Passengers will have a choice of 15 or more services a day in each direction, all offering high standards of on-board service and comfort.

Eurostar services will revolve around a core of specially-developed trains running between London and Paris in 3 hours, and London and Brussels in 3 hours and 15 minutes. There will also be direct Eurostar services from Scotland, the North and the Midlands to Paris and Brussels. The Channel Tunnel will also give many British business travellers their first taste of international sleeper trains. There will be a nightly service from London Waterloo (departing 21.00) to Cologne, Dortmund, Bonn and Frankfurt (arriving 07.40 in Frankfurt) with an additional service to Rotterdam, the Hague and Amsterdam, departing at 21.30 and arriving in Amsterdam at 08.30.

Will the business traveller benefit from the new competition in the international travel market, created by the opening of the Tunnel? Certainly, there will be benefits in terms of service quality: the frequency of the service, the speed and level of comfort. But the business community may be disappointed that prices for using the Tunnel are not likely to be that much lower than the cost of travelling by air from Britain to continental Europe. Even so, this should not come as a surprise. As early as 1992, those given the responsibility of operating trains through the Tunnel were predicting fares more or less in line with the cost of flying. Richard Edgley, then managing director of European Passenger Services (EPS), the British Rail subsidiary responsible for the British part of the new international services using the Tunnel, claimed:

> Our service will at least match and even better what our competitors can do. It will be faster by rail than air, city centre to city centre. So we don't think we will need to undercut air fares significantly.

In truth, the ability of EPS to trim fares will be severely restricted because of the high cost of the Eurostar trains, the toll for using the Channel Tunnel and extra operating costs incurred in running this service.

Link-ups with air transport

An important future trend in rail travel will be created by the need to provide link-ups between high-speed trains and air transport, to make connections between the two modes as convenient as possible. These already exist at the airports of Frankfurt, Schiphol, Zurich and Geneva, and will be followed by TGV links at Paris Charles de Gaulle and Lyon Satolas.

In Britain, the aspirations of airports such as Heathrow and Gatwick to be important hub and spoke operations would receive a vital boost from rail link-ups with future high-speed trains arriving through the Channel Tunnel. But, if the history of the Heathrow Link is anything to go by, that day is not exactly imminent. An express train service linking Heathrow airport with Paddington station in central London was finally given the go-ahead in Spring 1993, after several years of deliberation. The delays were caused by extended discussions between British Rail and the British Airports Authority as to who would pay for what.

Nevertheless, work started at the end of 1993, with a completion date of 1997. Four trains will run every hour from dedicated platforms at Heathrow and Paddington. The service will be operated by electric trains specially adapted to carry bulky luggage, and the journey will take around 16 minutes to Heathrow Terminals 1–3, while Terminal 4 will require an extra four minutes. Fares are expected to be about £9 one-way and £14 return (1993 prices).

CAR RENTAL

Several million car rental reservations are made in the UK each year, and the typical short-term rental customer is a business traveller picking up a car at an airport or railway station. It is at these termini that the names of the main car rental companies can be seen emblazoned over their distinctive counters: Europcar and Avis, Europe's biggest car rental companies, Hertz, the world's biggest, and Budget, are the names most familiar to frequent travellers. For the UK, the principal car rental companies' share of the market is shown in Figure 5.7.

Airport and rail-travel links are extremely important to car rental

Company	Market share %
Avis	12
Europcar	11
Eurodollar	9
Hertz	7
Budget	7
Others	54
Total	100%

Figure 5.7   UK car rental market share 1990/91
Source: P.D. Smith, *European Car Hire Industry*, Economist Intelligence Unit, 1992

companies. For example, 55 per cent of Avis' rental revenue comes from passengers arriving at (primarily, *international*) airports. The company has established formal links with many airlines, including Alitalia, SAS, Iberia and British Midland, in whose reservation offices Avis car rental services may also be booked.

Rail passengers are also a major source of interest for this company. In the early 1990s in France, Avis launched the service 'Train & Auto', which enables rail customers to book car rental when purchasing their train tickets. National railway staff deal entirely with the booking and the passenger collects his or her car on arrival by rail at the destination. Cars can be returned to the railway station at which they were picked up or at any of the other 200 principal railway stations in France.

Many companies regulate their employees' use of car rental when they are travelling on business. The American Express *Business Travel and Expense Management Report 1992* stated that 52 per cent of companies involved in its survey exercised a degree of control in this area of business travel. This can take several forms. American Express found that, of those companies with a policy concerning the use of car rental,

- 44% required employees to use a designated car hire agency

- 42% insisted on prior authorisation, and

- 27% only permitted car hire in an emergency.

Companies with large numbers of employees travelling regularly on business are often able to negotiate favourable corporate rates with car rental firms. The American Express survey found that 23 per cent of the companies interviewed had discounts arranged on car hire.

Trends

The period of strong growth enjoyed by the European car hire industry during the latter part of the 1980s had ground to a halt by 1992. Nowhere was this trend experienced more sharply than in the UK, where the number of car rental contracts fell dramatically as a result of the recession.

Precisely because of the economic downturn and the number of new companies entering the market, car hire firms had been extremely competitive in the early 1990s. It had become quicker, easier and cheaper for business travellers to rent cars, due to a plethora of inclusive deals and technical innovations.

A good example of innovation is seen in the speedier reservations systems and 'express' desks which most car rental companies introduced for their business clients, in order to save them time queuing.

For example, in 1993, Europcar introduced its new computer system, Greenway, to provide customers with an improved service, including expedited reservations and payment. A yield-management system controlled by the Greenway system was designed to guarantee customers the best rate at any given time, dependent on demand, length of rental, season and type of customer. This means that frequent users get priority and that rates are flexible, fixed according to demand.

Tiered check-in levels, similar to airlines' first, business and economy class check-in desks, were also introduced by Europcar. Customers not requiring personal service can now use an interactive, self-service car hire 'vending' machine. To use this, bookers insert their swipe card for identification and then choose from a menu of car types which appears on the screen; for those who have already made the booking, by telephone for example, confirmation of the reservation appears. After confirmation, a key is dropped from the machine and a diagram on the screen shows from which bay the car may be collected. On return, the customer simply keys into the machine his/her mileage and the amount of petrol left in the tank.

These innovations mean reduced costs of each transaction, reductions which can be passed on to the customer, giving Europcar an important advantage in a fiercely competitive market.

Another method which car rental companies are using to compete successfully is the introduction of reward schemes for frequent users, along the lines of schemes used by other sectors of the business travel industry. For example, there is the Avis Club. Membership guarantees the customer discounts of up to 30 per cent on standard rates, accelerated booking procedures and discounts in certain hotel chains, as well as a range of special offers throughout the year.

Future trends

Airports or railway stations?

Several car rental companies in Europe predict a decline in the importance of airports as a proportion of their overall market sources. As points of sale, airport locations are extremely expensive. The car rental companies are obliged to pay royalties to the airports, and this can be as high as 6–9 per cent of turnover. Also, they have to pay for the car parking places they need for their vehicles.

As a result, car rental companies are increasingly looking towards city-centre locations as sources of future business. Hertz, for example, with 30 per cent of the European airport market is now turning towards city centres as a source of bookings.

Railway termini, for example, are regarded as being potential growth areas, as train travel for business purposes increases in popularity. But, ironically, as high-speed trains bring passengers directly into city centres, there is a growing tendency for businesses to move to 'green field', out-of-town locations, away from the high rents, congestion and pollution of city centres. In the future, the typical business customer for short-term car rental may be a rail passenger arriving at a station and hiring a car to drive to his or her final, out-of-town destination.

Joint marketing schemes with hotels?

One possibility mooted by Peter Smith, the author of the Economist Intelligence Unit's report, the *European Car Hire Industry*, was that of joint marketing schemes between hotels and car rental firms. Through this arrangement, each partner would favour the services of the other as the 'preferred' provider of accommodation or hired cars, in much the same way as airlines have their preferred hotels at the destinations they serve. The report pointed out the potential mutual advantages of such schemes, which would bring a marked improvement to the current informal situation in which the choice of car rental firm usually depends on the whim of the hotel's hall porter.

Higher rates?

Ironically the recession itself, having been a contributory factor in reducing car hire rates during the early 1990s, may cause rates to rise again. This prediction was made in the January 1993 edition of *Business Traveller* magazine:

> Car hire companies' costs are based on two key items: their fleet and their personnel. They have received very high discounts over the last three or four years from car manufacturers, which have greatly reduced the cost of their fleet.

> 'What we see now is car manufacturers with significant losses, so they have changed their strategy in this area. They will restrict numbers of cars into our fleet so prices will be higher', warned Robin Davis, vice president of marketing and sales for Hertz Europe.

> The car hire companies will have to keep their cars for slightly longer and pass on some of the cost to the consumer. Hertz reckons the price rise will be in the region of 5%–10% across all categories.

More standardisation?

The EIU report drew attention to the fact that, in the UK in particular, travel agency staff are generally very uninformed about car rental, and that the industry as a whole was doing very little to educate them. While computer reservations systems (see Chapter 7) will make it easier for travel agents to book car hire for customers, there will still be a need for greater transparency in this industry.

Compared to the airline industry with its standard price codes and classification systems (first class, business, economy), the car hire companies still lack this degree of standardisation. Moves to rectify this situation would greatly facilitate the performance of travel agents *vis-à-vis* the car rental industry. There is good reason to believe, therefore, that there will be increasing pressure upon car rental companies to simplify their pricing structure and introduce some degree of rationalisation of their systems in the future.

SEA TRAVEL

For island nations such as the UK, the sea has been used for the purpose of business travel ever since the first ships set off to trade in distant lands, in the earliest days of international commerce. But, with the invention of the passenger aircraft, sea travel inevitably declined in importance as business travellers were seduced by the speed and glamour of international jet travel.

Nevertheless, sea travel for business survives in one form at least: the car ferries. And the construction of the Channel Tunnel, far from sounding the death knell of these ferries, has stimulated the ferry operators to develop new, attractive and efficient services in order to face up to this competition. Many of the features of the new generation of car ferries have been designed with the business traveller in mind.

P&O European Ferries, for example, now offers five 'superferries' and has installed new technology enabling faster check-ins to improve speed and efficiency. With P&O's new computerised ticketing process plus an improved loading system at Dover, motorists need arrive at Dover only 20 minutes before sailing. Both Sealink and P&O have also increased the number of crossings on their Dover–Calais route, with departures hourly and every 45 minutes, respectively.

P&O European Ferries is the only car ferry operator to offer Club Class service, available for a small supplement. For that, business travellers travel in their own Club Class lounge, with complimentary tea and coffee and newspapers. On the crossings from Dover and on the Larne–Cairnryan service, Club Class passengers also have available to them desks in quiet corners, with telephone, fax and photocopying facilities. P&O ships from Portsmouth to Le Havre and Cherbourg even offer day cabins for confidential meetings.

In short, the ferry operators are fighting back, determined to face up to the new competition for the business traveller to or from the British mainland.

But some see even brighter prospects for sea-borne business travellers in the years to come. Charles Owen, principal consultant with Tourism by Design, has a vision of a revival of transatlantic ocean-liner travel as one means of combining business with pleasure:

> Scheduled sea travel . . . car ferries apart, has long been in decline and, as the most civilised and sumptuous form of travel yet devised, more's the pity. On some of the once busiest routes, notably Western Europe to New York, plied today some dozen times a year by *QE2*, itself no stranger to the conference business, incentive travel could well spark a renaissance.

> Ships of that ilk are, in effect, grand hotels afloat and, given the same up-to-date facilities for business people and, for those in a hurry, the option of one way by air, they can fulfil a similar serious-minded purpose while conveying their customers in romantic yet work-inducing splendour towards their promised lands. What chance that our successors, the next generation of business tourists, having challenged the supremacy and the claustrophobic, pollution-spreading aeroplane, will take gleefully, once more, to a life on the ocean wave?

> *Tourism Management*, Vol. 13, No. 2, June 1992

WOMEN TRAVELLERS

As more and more women travel on business, how does their experience as passengers compare with the promises of smiling service and privileged pampering implied by the transport operators' advertising? Less well than the experience of their male colleagues, by many accounts.

In the *Daily Telegraph* of 28 November, 1992, Edward Welsh reported the experience of one female executive traveller as follows:

> After a three-day business trip in America, Gill Feaster was looking forward to some peace and quiet in the executive lounge of a US airline before catching her flight home to London. But instead of receiving a warm welcome, she was treated like a gatecrasher. 'A hostess shouted across the room, "This is for business class passengers only", and then demanded to see my ticket', said the fashion designer, who had paid the

appropriate fare. 'I didn't see one businessman entering the lounge who was questioned. Women travellers don't get the same respect.'

A 1992 survey by Mintel, the market research analysts, concluded that the attitudes of airline staff towards women needed to be improved: 'It would seem to be an area that deserves more attention, as airlines cannot afford to alienate a group so fundamental as women.'

Many of Mintel's findings are echoed by the Businesswoman's Travel Club, whose members have a catalogue of complaints against the airlines: male-orientated in-flight magazines, masculine amenity bags, less attentive service for women, check-in staff who believe that women are more tolerant than men about sitting next to crying babies, and airline staff's assumption that if a woman is travelling with a man he must be her husband or boss.

Gill Upton, editor-in-chief of *Business Traveller* magazine, believes that an airline's treatment of female air travellers often reflects either the culture of a carrier's home country or the age of the female cabin crew:

> The worst problems are on the Asian carriers. The cabin crew go to a smile school where they get taught to fawn over men and ignore the women. You sit next to a man and he gets second helpings, his pillow puffed up and extra champagne.

According to Upton, where there is a problem with American or European airlines in this respect, it is because 'older stewardesses put down women who are doing better than they are'. She recommends Virgin Atlantic cabin crews, younger than on most carriers, for treating men and women equally.

However, while most women air travellers would admit that airlines have changed for the better during the past decade, Ros Martin, the Businesswoman's Travel Club's general manager, feels carriers still have a long way to go: 'They are becoming more aware of women travellers. But there has to be more staff training concerning the attitude of cabin crew.'

....

Questions   1 What kinds of incentive do airlines offer their clients in order to persuade them to travel first class or business class?

2 What innovations have car hire companies made in order to attract clients?

3 What are the pros and cons of train sleeper services for business travellers?

Assignments 1 Collect a number of newspapers and magazines from the travel trade press. Cut out examples of advertisements placed by transport operators and aimed at the business traveller. Compile a chart noting, for each advertisement, the claims the operator makes for its service under each of the following headings: Speed, Comfort, Reliability and Punctuality, Convenience, Frequency, Value for money.

2 Most termini, such as airports and train stations, offer special facilities for business passengers. Arrange a visit to a transport terminal, in order to see these facilities for yourself. Write a report on your findings.

Key terms Before moving on to the next chapter, make sure you understand the meaning of the following terms:

Seat pitch and configuration

Frequent flyer schemes

In-flight technology

Airport lounges

Hub-and-spoke operation

6

Business tourism accommodation

INTRODUCTION

Hotels provide the vast majority of the accommodation for those travelling on business, attending conferences and exhibitions or participating in incentive trips. In the UK, hotels and guest houses between them account for two-thirds of all business tourism accommodation. Only universities (mainly for conferences) and friends and family provide any other significant forms of accommodation.

Few hotels in the UK could survive on their leisure clientele alone. Particularly in city locations, hotels depend on high-spending business guests to fill their rooms from Monday to Friday. Only when the weekend arrives do many hotels cut their rates for the leisure market, with special weekend deals.

A company or an exhibition or conference organiser may be able to negotiate a special corporate or conference rate with hoteliers, if they guarantee an adequate volume of guests. But providing for the business client presents a number of challenges to hotel owners.

Business guests make their own particular demands on hotels. What do hotels have to provide in order to cater successfully for this distinctive market?

High standards

It is rare to find business guests in hotels of below the grade of 2 stars. This is partly a case of guests' personal standards and their idea of what they 'deserve', and partly because executives staying in a Bed & Breakfast, for example, would have a severe credibility problem with those they had come to do business with. Also, the range of services which business travellers expect from the providers of their accommodation are only found at the upper end of the market.

But those travelling for business purposes on behalf of the companies they work for often have no choice as to which hotel or grade of hotel they use. This is because many companies have written rules or guidelines relating to their employees' use of hotel accommodation. This was found to be the case for 47 per cent of companies described in the American Express *Business Travel and Expense Management Report 1992*. Of the companies participating in the survey, 39 per cent actually stipulated that certain hotels had to be used by their travelling executives – usually those hotels with which the companies had negotiated a corporate rate or special discount. (The difference between the two percentages suggests that a sizeable number of companies do not insist on employees using the very hotels with which favourable rates have been specially negotiated.)

As in the case of class of air and train travel, management grade is an important factor in determining the level of accommodation to which business travellers are entitled, when their companies are paying. Figure 6.1 shows how companies' rules on grade of hotel operate.

	Board directors	Senior managers	Middle and junior managers
Five star	49%	14%	4%
Four star	28%	39%	17%
Three star	11%	33%	42%
Two star	2%	3%	13%
Depends/variable	10%	11%	24%

Base: Companies with hotel rules.

Figure 6.1   Grades of hotel allowed for different management grades
Source: *Business Travel & Expense Management Report 1992*, published by American Express Europe Ltd

Business facilities

For the business guest, the hotel is often an extension of his or her office – a place where he or she may have to do some work. Such guests may need to have something typed, faxed or translated, often at short notice, and good business hotels can arrange this. Many have their own Business Centres – in some cases an entire floor where services of this kind are provided or where the business guest can have the use of a personal computer, for example.

For the business market, keeping in touch is much more important than it is for holidaymakers or leisure travellers. Incoming messages for the business guest must be transmitted quickly and accurately.

But the telephone is the essential piece of equipment for those travelling on business, particularly overseas. A survey by the American telephone company AT&T in the early 1990s showed that 20 per cent of British businesspeople spend over £1,000 a year each on phone calls while abroad. This is an area of contention between the business traveller and hotels.

The same survey also discovered that 68 per cent of businesspeople make their phone calls from hotels and that hotel phone surcharges were given the third highest 'hassle rating' after airports and airlines, by business travellers.

Hotels impose mark-ups on call costs of between 500 and 800 per cent, according to the April 1993 edition of *Business Traveller* magazine. The justification normally given by the hotels themselves is that these charges are necessary to offset the cost of the hotel switchboard and the multiple telephone lines which ensure guests always have a telephone line available to them. Travellers wishing to avoid paying these charges have several options open to them. Some use post offices or telephone boxes and payphones to make their calls. But this can involve juggling with a lot of loose change in a foreign currency – not always practical.

Another option which is being increasingly adopted by business travellers is the use of telephone *calling cards*. These allow guests to phone from their rooms without paying the often exorbitant prices charged by hotels for using their lines. Calling cards are issued by telephone companies such as AT&T and Sprint in the US and BT and Mercury in the UK, as well as independent firms such as World Telecard and

Interglobe. The cards are issued either free of charge or for a small fee, and calls made using them are subsequently debited to the caller's credit card or charge card, by the telephone company.

Health facilities

With the general interest in sport and health at an all-time high level, those who spend much of their day sitting in meetings or trains and having heavy business lunches are increasingly looking for accommodation with facilities to help keep them in shape. Hotels have responded by adding swimming pools, work-out rooms, and other health facilities. Not only do these attract the business market, but they also help when promoting the hotel to potential weekend leisure guests.

An outstanding example of this came in 1993, when London's Savoy hotel opened its new Fitness Gallery. Open initially to residents only, this comprises a rooftop swimming pool, gym, sauna, massage and steam rooms.

Dining facilities

How can those in charge of hotels' dining facilities be most responsive to business travellers' needs?

They ought to begin by noticing that the popular image of the business traveller as a florid, opulent old gent who enjoys tucking into a five-course dinner, is now largely out of date. Today's business travellers are often younger, leaner and fitter than those of a few decades ago, and they are keen to remain that way. This they can only do by eschewing gastronomic self-indulgence and eating in a healthy, balanced way.

Fortunately, the message appears to be getting through: according to Goff's *Business Traveller's Guide*, former favourites, rich with heart-stopping ingredients, such as tournedos rossine, *homard à l'americaine* and peach melba are now seldom featured, at least on day-time menus, relatively down-to-earth country dishes or salads being a more usual fare.

Another characteristic of business guests is that, unless they are travelling as part of a group, they are likely to be eating alone. The better hotels will successfully make the solitary diner feel relaxed and looked after; others will make him or her feel like a second class customer. Why?

There are several reasons why restaurant staff can bear a grudge against those eating alone. Firstly, the single restaurant customer takes up a whole table, a fact resented by busy restaurants if they have to turn away groups because every table is taken; secondly, single customers tend to consume less than those eating in pairs or in groups, since there is no 'egging-on' factor ('Shall we have another bottle of wine?' 'Go on. And I'll have cheese *and* a dessert if you will . . .'); finally, women dining alone still tend to be frowned upon by restaurant managers obsessed by the 'respectability' of their establishments, and for this reason, such customers often find themselves tucked out of sight in no man's land beside the toilets or the entrance to the kitchen.

'Hostess' facilities

In the late 1980s, the MP Edwina Currie recommended British business-men to take a good book with them while travelling abroad on business trips. The idea was that this would give them something to curl up in bed with at the end of their working day – something which would not seriously endanger their own health and that of their partners.

Nevertheless, despite these exhortations, many hotels remain convinced that the pleasures of the flesh are an essential part of any business trip, and many of them attempt to cater for this need accordingly. Visitors to Third World countries return with stories of finding by their hotel bed, not Gideon's Bible, but an illustrated catalogue of 'masseuses' who will visit guests' rooms – for the right fee.

But this phenomenon is not at all unknown in the developed world too, where many prestigious hotels include the euphemistically-named 'hostess bar' among their services for guests. The best motto for guests tempted to enjoy the services of a Thai masseuse or Mayfair hostess must surely be *caveat emptor*.

AIRPORT BUSINESS HOTELS

Originally, airport hotels were built to cater for the 'one night transit' client – travellers having an overnight stop before, after, or in between flights.

But since the mid-1970s, airport hotel business throughout Western Europe has expanded dramatically, due mainly to a considerable increase in non-airport-related business.

During that period, there has been a trend among companies of all kinds to relocate near to airports, for ease of access to the outside world and to escape the high rents and traffic congestion of city-centre locations. Hoteliers have aimed to serve this new market by developing their properties to city-centre standards. The success of this strategy has been astonishing: airport hotels' occupancy rates are well above average in most cases (typically 10 to 30 per cent higher than those of their city-centre counterparts, according to Alex McWhirter, writing in the June 1993 edition of *Business Traveller* magazine); and, since there are no handy restaurants or bars in the vicinity apart from the hotels' own, guests are captive customers for the airport hotels' food and beverage outlets. All of this means that when times are tough in the business, airport hotels tend to fare better than others.

A good illustration of this are the airport hotels in Brussels, which receive windfall business from the several dozen multinationals located nearby. The Holiday Inn, for example, claims an average occupancy rate of just under 70 per cent year round (which means that it is virtually full during the working week), compared with the 50 per cent occupancy rates seen in central Brussels. At Heathrow, despite a supply of 8,000 rooms near the airport, occupancy rates there are also much higher than in central London. Winter-time occupancy at the 840-room Forte Excelsior runs at between 72 and 83 per cent, compared to central London, where equivalent leading properties are lucky to achieve 60 per cent.

Such levels of business have meant that every major hotel chain is now actively developing airport properties in Western Europe. Munich got its own Kempinski in 1994, while Paris Charles de Gaulle, boasting its futuristic interchange with the high-speed TGV rail station, was seeing Meridien, Hyatt and Hilton building hotels at the airport. Paris' first sizeable airport hotel, the Hyatt, would, in the words of its director, be 'dramatic, controversial, ultramodern'. The 400 rooms will include 80 executive rooms, conference facilities, business and fitness centres and a 'fun pub' centre, offering everything from darts to disco. The hotel plans to work closely with the airlines on special deals for business travellers.

But the expansion in airport hotels has been, for the main part, independent of airport traffic. Local business, from companies with their premises near the airport, and the conference market are both being very successfully tapped. With budgets for holding conferences continuing to shrink, hotels with easy access to airports are becoming increasingly popular for this kind of event. For example, Heathrow's Sheraton Skyline, where 30 per cent of business is conference-related, can accommodate up to 400 delegates. The winner of the *Executive Travel*/Utell International Best Conference Hotel for eight out of the nine years leading up to 1993 is another Heathrow property, the 636-room Penta Hotel (now the Ramada Hotel Heathrow). Facilities there include a theatre, 30 different sizes of meeting room and professional technicians.

The product itself has, in many cases, been adapted to appeal to a wider business market. As Alex McWhirter, the *Business Traveller* journalist, pointed out in June 1993:

> Executive floors and fitness centres are now commonplace among the better properties. Some hotels are adding other facilities for fitness freaks, like jogging tracks and small golf courses. Food and beverage outlets are moving beyond the obvious themes: Forte properties at Heathrow have brought in a Chinese restaurant, plus UK high street outlets like Carvery and Wheelers. And in innumerable cases, hotels even provide transfers to downtown or to nearby companies.

To add further to their appeal, many airport hotels offer corporate discounts, special weekend deals, and free parking while their guests are away.

With the airport hotel trend set to continue, it is certainly worth watching to see if many European airports go the way of Frankfurt. There, it is a fairly common phenomenon for business executives to fly in, get a special deal at the Sheraton and fly out again, without actually going into the city itself!

CASE
STUDY

The Berkeley

One of London's top three hotels, the Berkeley, which is part of the Savoy Group of Hotels and Restaurants, prides itself on providing its business guests with a service which combines discretion with efficiency.

This is how the hotel describes its services for business guests:

Business services

Business guests' welcome to the Berkeley begins long before they are greeted by the doorman on arrival at the hotel. Those arriving at London airport are personally met by an employee of the Savoy Group, wearing the distinctive blue frock coat and peaked cap, which has characterised these 'meeters and greeters' ever since Heathrow opened some 40 years ago. Their job is to welcome guests and usher them to their pre-booked, chauffeur-driven cars, self-drive cars or taxis, and then to telephone the Berkeley to alert the hotel of their estimated time of arrival.

Once at the hotel, the multi-lingual reception staff take over. The Savoy Group has a policy of employing bi-lingual or multi-lingual receptionists, to help the overseas business guest feel at home.

Rooms at the Berkeley have been designed with the needs of the business guest in mind. Video-players are provided in all rooms and suites, enabling them to be used for small business presentations. However, the Berkeley has not followed other hotels in creating a special business centre in the hotel. The company's Managing Director Giles Shepard explains why: 'Our guests appreciate discretion and privacy, which is why we have deliberately avoided the installation of business centres, where these cannot be guaranteed.'

Instead, travelling executives have available to them a 'mobile business centre' which contains a fax machine, laptop computer, printer and modem. This can be wheeled into the guest's room whenever it is required. Secretarial and typing services are arranged promptly and efficiently by the hotel's concierge, who can also arrange everything else the business guest is likely to require: translators, interpreters, theatre tickets or restaurant bookings. Mobile telephones are also available on request.

Meeting rooms

Each of the meeting rooms at the Berkeley has been imaginatively decorated and furnished to produce its own unique but essentially English personality. Reflections from its mirrored ceiling and crystal chandeliers enhance the elegance of the *Ballroom*, for example. With its own private entrance, via a spectacular interior marquee, the Ballroom provides a glittering backdrop to receptions, banquets and luncheons, for up to 450 guests for cocktails and between 70 and 180 for luncheon or dinner. The *Crystal Room*, adjoining the Ballroom, is highly versatile for both business and social gatherings. Up to 50 guests can be accommodated in theatre-style seating, adjourning to one of the neighbouring private rooms for luncheon or dinner.

In addition to several other smaller meeting rooms, the Berkeley also has its own exclusive in-house cinema, The Minema. Adjoining the hotel, this has its own separate entrance off Knightsbridge, and can be used for private screenings, lectures and conferences, for up to 68 people.

Additional services

The *health facilities* available include a gymnasium and rooftop swimming pool that is open from 07.00 to 20.00 hrs so that the health-conscious can work out before and after work. Stress-reducing beauty and body treatments including massages, aromatherapy and reflexology are available in the hotel's beauty centre.

The hotel's *maître d's*, used to welcoming single diners, make a point of making them feel comfortable in the restaurants. And to woo the business-woman, there are specially equipped rooms, female bar staff and a female security chief.

For departing business guests, the Berkeley hall porter telephones through details, and at the airport, the guests are met and their departure formalities dealt with, reducing possible stress and strains to a minimum.

Incentives

The Savoy Group as a whole specialises in individually-tailored incentive programmes for small groups: 'fascinating visits to the most intriguing locations, introductions to people and places not normally encountered, and events to make the experience unforgettable.'

Among the possibilities available in London are:

● a chance to take 'Breakfast at Tiffany's' in the boardroom of the famous jeweller in Old Bond Street, followed by a personal tour of the store with a commentary on the displays of precious stones and exclusive jewellery;

● shopping at Harrods, after hours, in complete privacy;

● through a private arrangement with the Household Cavalry Mounted Regiment, the chance to drive through the grounds of Windsor Great Park in a horse-drawn carriage accompanied by liveried grooms.

SPECIAL PACKAGES – THE COPACABANA PALACE HOTEL

In the battle to attract business clients and turn them into loyal customers, many hotels offer both special packages and reduced rates for guests staying on business trips. A good example of this is the Copacabana Palace Hotel in Rio de Janeiro. This hotel, one of Brazil's grandest institutions, was where 14 heads of state, including the British Prime Minister, stayed during the 1992 Earth Summit Conference in Rio. But even for the ordinary businessman or woman, the Copacabana Palace offers an impressive range of services – at an advantageous price. The hotel's all-inclusive Executive Portfolio rate of $160 per night entitles business guests to personal attention from the moment they arrive in the city. One of the hotel's limousines awaits those arriving at Rio's airport, with a chauffeur and a member of the hotel's multi-lingual Customer Relations team, as part of the 'Meet and Greet service'. The limousine remains at their disposal during their stay, for transport to meetings in the city's business district, five or six kilometres away from Copacabana Beach. The Executive Portfolio rate also entitles guests to wordprocessing, fax, telex, and photocopying services, as well as a daily newspaper. Figure 6.2 shows an example of the Copacabana Palace Hotel's publicity for this service. Figure 6.3 shows Copacabana Beach by night.

COPACABANA PALACE
RIO DE JANEIRO · BRAZIL

$160 MEANS A GREAT DEAL TO
BUSINESS TRAVELLERS

If you are travelling to Rio on business, start by making the best deal in town - at the
Copacabana Palace. For the new Executive Portfolio rate of $160 (plus 10% service charge), you
can enjoy the comfort, prestige and superb facilities of Rio's premier business hotel.
The Copacabana Palace is ideally situated not only on Rio's most famous beach, but also
just ten minutes from the downtown business district, and offers everything you need to make
your stay successful and enjoyable.

EXECUTIVE
PORTFOLIO

FIRST CLASS FOR BUSINESS

Figure 6.2   Copacabana Palace Hotel publicity leaflet

Figure 6.3   Copacabana Beach, Rio de Janeiro, by night
© Stuart Crawshaw

HOTEL LOYALTY CLUBS

That business guests are lucrative customers for hotels is in no doubt. Not only do they pay a valuable mid-week room rate, but they are also more likely to patronise the hotel's food and beverage outlets.

Hotels have therefore followed in the footsteps of airlines and car rental companies in creating loyalty clubs for the frequent traveller, with the aim of keeping the business coming in from this valuable and valued segment of their clientele.

These clubs offer many advantages to the business traveller. Not only is membership usually free, but its benefits can translate into substantial savings of both time and money. Some of the benefits on offer were listed by Alex McWhirter in his article on this subject for *Business Traveller*'s December 1991 edition.

For example, the late check-out or early check-in facility offered to certain hotel club cardholders can avoid the expense of paying for an extra night's accommodation; express check-in/check-out facilities make for valuable time savings; and the possibility of receiving free room upgrades – another widespread benefit of membership – is another worthwhile perk. Hotel loyalty club members can also benefit from a wide range of other privileges, from the promise of a room always being available (even when the hotel is fully-booked for 'normal' guests) to discounts on laundry and telephone call surcharges, and complimentary items such as fruit baskets and newspapers. But perhaps the greatest advantage to the member is that of being accorded VIP status throughout his or her stay in the hotel.

The keeping of members' 'guest histories', along with their preferences regarding room position, morning newspaper, and even toiletries and minibar contents, are usually another feature of hotel loyalty clubs. For example, the Hilton Club for frequent business travellers, introduced in 1990, now has around 7,000 members. A database of members' preferences ensures that loyal guests get recognition and precise personal service in whichever Hilton they use, worldwide.

A good example of a hotel loyalty club is Forte's Crest Club. Forte promotes its 28 Crest properties as definite business hotels, having, during 1992, upgraded all bedrooms to include desks and computer modems. Along with 24-hour room service, other business services include complimentary message pagers, free newspapers and business magazines, and secretarial back-up. Guests who are not satisfied that the four-star Crest chain lives up to its promise of 'Business Class Satisfaction Guaranteed' may claim a night's free accommodation.

In 1993, Forte Hotels launched its Crest Club designed exclusively for frequent business guests, offering them free family weekends on a points-based scheme. Once members have registered at the hotel, they receive a card, which must then be presented whenever they check in at Crest hotels, to earn points. Regular guests earn one point for each overnight stay, while corporate clients earn two. When ten points have been accumulated, the guest may choose one free night's accommodation from Friday to Sunday. Meals are not included, but partners and a maximum of two children under 16 stay free.

WOMEN AS HOTEL BUSINESS GUESTS

What kind of treatment do female business guests receive in hotels? What kind of messages are being sent to this important segment of the business tourism market by hotels rushing to install hostess bars, body-building equipment and trouser presses? The evidence suggests that many single women find staying in a top hotel as intimidating as a crusty gentlemen's club.

In 1992, *ELLE* magazine sent six female journalists undercover into six of the UK's grandest hotel establishments to check out the reaction when a woman, staying alone, requests various services. The results demonstrate some of the problems faced by female hotel guests, as well as showing some of the demands which business travellers in general make upon hotel services.

Is there a message for me?

The journalists asked this question on checking into the hotels, at 7pm. The same message had been left for all of them:

This is Véronique from Azzedine Alaïa. He has your new dress ready in the Paris salon. Could you telephone me at the Bistro-cave Envierges before 6pm or tomorrow at Le Casbah after 8pm?

The Dorchester: Message given on arrival. Spelling mistake – 'El Casbha'.

The Hilton: No message handed over.

The Savoy: Perfect message given on arrival.

The Connaught: Message given on arrival. Spelling mistakes – 'Azzaldine' and 'Lenouque'.

The Ritz: Message given on arrival. Accurate apart from spelling of 'Enzierges'.

The Balmoral, Edinburgh: Message given on arrival. Spelling mistake – 'Le Cafbah'.

I've got a simple business letter that needs translating into Italian.

The Dorchester: 'If you want a professional translation, it is too late (7.15pm) to do it today. However, we have some Italian experts here who could help.' Translation arrived within an hour.

The Hilton: 'Go to the business floor.' No one on duty to translate into Italian. Offered outside service. Then a member of staff who has A-level Italian offered to translate. Translation arrived the following morning.

The Savoy: 'Ask our Italian concierge.' He was very helpful, completed it within an hour, and chatted about his birthplace.

The Connaught: 'No problem.' Translation arrived at 11pm.

The Ritz: 'Yes.' Translation arrived in one hour.

The Balmoral: 'Translations are dealt with in our business centre from 8am to 6pm only.'

I don't like the room. Can I have another one?

The Dorchester: Without asking, I was upgraded to a large double room on the top floor.

The Hilton: 'No problem.' Upgraded to a large double room on 'the luxury (27th) floor' at no extra charge.

The Savoy: Offered another room but was not upgraded.

The Connaught: 'It is no problem at all.' New room was larger, with a better view.

The Ritz: 'Only our suites overlook the park.' Not offered an upgraded room.

The Balmoral: 'No. We are absolutely full.' (This was true.)

Can you get me a table at Le Caprice tonight at 9pm?

The Dorchester: Rang back in three minutes. 'Unfortunately, they are fully booked. My apologies, madam.'

The Hilton: 'Only one seat at the bar available.'

The Savoy: 'Will that be a table for one?' A few minutes later reported, 'I can only get you a seat at the bar at 10pm.'

The Connaught: Not at Le Caprice, but the porter suggested The Ivy 'which is under the same management'. Full marks for ingenuity.

The Ritz: 'I can only get you a seat at the bar at 10pm.'

The Balmoral: n/a.

Drinks alone at the bar/foyer around 7.30pm.

The Dorchester: 'Would you like to sit by the piano?' One male guest stared at me throughout. Atmosphere like a dark cocktail bar. I felt uncomfortable on my own. Moved to well-lit foyer.

The Hilton: Very fast service. I felt comfortable by myself.

The Savoy: Waiter very attentive. 'Are you on your own or are you waiting for someone? Do you require a table for dinner on your own?'

The Connaught: 'A table for two is waiting for you.' I explained I was by myself. 'Oh, I'm so sorry madam.'

The Ritz: I ordered a vodka and Slimline tonic. When it arrived the tonic wasn't Slimline so I sent it back.

The Balmoral: A corporate Kwik-Fit dinner meant that the small bar was packed and claustrophobic. Large glasses of champagne but a depressing atmosphere.

Do you have any condoms?

The Dorchester: 'Yes, I could get you some. Just ring me if you want them.'

The Hilton: 'How many would you like?' Three. Five minutes later, 'We only have packs of 12.' Arrived within three minutes.

The Savoy: 'I'm sorry? Condoms? No madam, I don't think so.'

The Connaught: 'I'll ask the housekeeper and she can ask the porter to go to one of the men's lavatories. I'll get them from her and then no one need know who asked.' One pack of three was out-of-date, and, in the other, a packet of 12, only four were left.

The Ritz: The switchboard operator informed the hall porter. Ten minutes later, a packet of three Durex Elite arrived.

The Balmoral: 'Any particular size or colour?' In ten minutes, a packet of three Durex Ribbed Safe Play arrived.

In the restaurant for dinner: 'I'm on a diet. What would you suggest for about 600 calories?'

The Dorchester: Given a secluded table. 'Do you eat fish? What about grilled sole, vegetables with no butter and a salad without dressing? I don't know how many calories that would be. I must buy a calorie book.'

The Hilton: Asked for window table. Given a table near the kitchen entrance. Waiter helpful, but clearly knew nothing about diets. Settled on scallops with ratatouille (minus croutons), grilled sole with vegetables.

The Savoy: Room service. 'Have you looked at the menu . . . can you drink alcohol on the diet?' Suggested one glass of white wine and a dish of ratatouille on a bed of mashed potato. Portion tiny.

The Connaught: 'Oh, no, the chef would have no idea about 600 calories. What about poached turbot and steamed vegetables?' Two businessmen on an adjacent table stared at me constantly for an hour. Overheard: 'Do you think she's married?'

> **The Ritz**: 'I will consult the chef.' The result – asparagus vinaigrette, two tiny steaks and vegetables, and fresh berries for dessert.
>
> **The Balmoral**: Room service. 'What about a salmon sandwich? I suppose you won't want any butter on that.' Smoked salmon on white toast without butter and a large portion of crisps.

(The above extract is reprinted by kind permission of ELLE magazine.)

What can be done to improve the quality of the experience of women whose work obliges them to stay in hotels?

In 1992, Elizabeth Peacock, MP, on behalf of the Meetings Industry Association, carried out research into the needs of women attending conferences and other types of meeting requiring hotel accommodation.

Among the issues raised by the women decision makers whose views she sought were the need for lighter menus (to suit men as well as women), as well as the provision of special bedroom amenities including long mirrors, ironing boards, hairdryers and skirt hangers. However, Mrs Peacock emphasised that *security* considerations were 'now considered the most crucial area of concern'. According to her, 'musts' included the need for spy-holes in doors, the avoidance of large bedroom keys with the number on, and the allocation of rooms near lifts, avoiding the necessity to walk down long corridors. The availability of porters to collect and park cars was another firm recommendation, together with the designation of separate areas in restaurants for privacy and discretion.

CURRENT TRENDS

Supply and demand – hotels' meetings facilities

Many hotel groups are looking to the meetings market to improve occupancy rates and put them back on the road to recovery. The importance of this market is indicated by the fact that for several hotel groups, it forms more than 50 per cent of their total business. According to Queens Moat Houses, one of the largest British hotel groups specialising in services to business travellers, 80 per cent of their business is meetings-related. At the other end of the scale, one of

Britain's smallest hotel groups, Hidden Hotels, whose hotels are all secluded country house properties, is another example of a consortium specifically targeting the meetings sector. The conference and meetings industry provides 90 per cent of their business.

Such was the enthusiasm of hotels to cater for the conference market during the 'boom' period of the late 1980s that by the 1990s, there was growing awareness that the volume of meetings facilities available in UK hotels far outstripped demand.

This overchoice on the supply side inevitably led to buyers seeking more 'competitively priced' meetings packages from hotels. 'Shopping around' and sometimes leaving the booking decision until the very last moment (when bargains are to be had) has had an extremely detrimental effect on the hotel meetings industry.

In Spring 1992, *Conference & Incentive Travel* magazine reported that, as a result of oversupply, ' . . . hotels have been forced to discount prices in order to remain competitive. This is one of the main causes for concern among hotel operators, who feel that in the long run this will have adverse effects on quality.' Hoteliers were well aware that rates which are too cheap can have detrimental effects on service and quality, as well as training and investment for the future.

Not only have meetings buying patterns changed, the actual volume of business has also been hit by the depressed state of the economy. At the onset of the recession, 1991/92, UK hotels were already feeling the pinch. Fewer overseas customers and reductions in the size and length of meetings were reported by most hotel groups. In that single year, Rank Hotels saw their meetings business cut by 20 per cent, with a 33 per cent fall in the duration of meetings. All of their hotels reported fewer overnight conferences and less leisure time built into meetings. In the same period, Ramada International noted a drop in the average length of meetings and the number of those attending events held in their hotels.

Supply and demand – hotel accommodation

Oversupply in hotel meetings facilities was paralleled by a similar tendency regarding hotel rooms for accommodation.

In an article by Touche Ross Management Consultants which appeared in the January 1993 edition of the trade publication *Insights*, the authors said that one reason for the slump in hotel revenues was the dramatic growth in UK hotel bedroom stock beginning during the latter half of the 1980s, stimulated by the 'boom economy' of 1986–88, and continuing until 1992.

This led to the market moving decidedly in favour of buyers, at a time when recession in the UK was forcing corporate hotel users to cut back on travel expenses and subsidiary hotel uses, such as meetings and conferences. Beginning during the Gulf War, when hotel occupancy rates in general fell rapidly, there was a growing awareness among buyers that the official, published room rates were not immutable, and that, through negotiation, these could be substantially reduced in many cases. According to a 1992 survey by Horwarth, the hotel and leisure consultants,

> A discount culture prevails among consumers, and published tariffs continue to show significant disparities when compared with achieved room rates.

The prevalence of this 'discount culture' was in part encouraged by the pressure on many businesses to reduce their expenditure on hotel accommodation for their travelling employees. Travel managers generally recognise that it is easier to cut back on hotel costs than to reduce the cost of flying, for example, since there is usually a greater variety of hotel rates than air fares.

One result of this was that hotels' business customers were increasingly enquiring about *corporate rates*, which can be 10 per cent less than the posted price in many cases. Several factors can increase the chances of corporate customers, large and small, being given the lower rates for hotel accommodation. Two of the most important are:

1 *Customer loyalty*: The more a company uses a hotel, the more likely it is to get a discount. Therefore, it is very much in companies' interests to reduce the number of hotels they use in any one city, ensuring that more employees stay in a more restricted number of hotels.

2 *When customers use hotels*: Companies which use hotels during the lean periods of December and January, for example, are in a better position to strike good deals for the year as a whole than businesses which only use hotels during busy periods.

Trading down

Trading down is as prevalent in the accommodation sector as it is in transport. The Horwarth survey quoted above found firm evidence of business travellers staying in cheaper hotels.

Nevertheless, it seems unlikely that companies will ever abandon expensive hotels completely, for the simple reason that they would worry that customers and potential customers might not take their employees seriously if the latter were staying in more modest accommodation. However, it would not be unreasonable for companies to decide in the future which of their employees actually *need* to stay in expensive hotels and which could stay in cheaper establishments without affecting the standing of the company or their own credibility.

Meanwhile, the hotels most likely to benefit from the current economy measures instigated by companies are the mid-range, mid-priced properties which offer executives everything they are looking for at a price their companies can afford. For example, Holiday Inn Worldwide have in recent years seen their occupancy levels and profits boosted as executives move from the luxury end of the market to these hotels with a mid-market appeal.

Also, more and more hotels are putting together packages for the budget-conscious business traveller. An example is the InterContinental chain, with its Business Options scheme, launched in 1993. Customers paying the corporate rate can request Business Options, when making a reservation. This gives them the possibility of then choosing one benefit from the following: a suite upgrade, 25 per cent allowance on food and beverage bills, a second room for half price, free car parking, or double loyalty club points. Such schemes represent an important asset in the battle for the recession-hit business hotel guest.

FUTURE TRENDS

Information technology

Great scope exists for the use of information technology by hotels. This would directly benefit the business guest by offering considerable efficiency gains.

According to a MORI survey carried out in 1992, 70 per cent of the British hotel chains polled were not linked to a computer reservations system (CRS), and only half were using computerised property management systems, which allocate rooms to guests and keep track of housekeeping, maintenance and supplies.

Hotels are increasingly becoming aware of the potential offered by linking up with the airline-owned ticket reservation systems. Direct on-line links with these CRSs represent an important supplementary reservations system for hotels. With direct links through CRSs, confirmation of room requests is instantaneous, eliminating the need for fax and telex messages, which can go astray.

In an interview reported by Peter Miller in the *Financial Times* of 25 September, 1992, Carl Holton, head of marketing for Galileo, the predominant airline computer reservations system in the UK, predicted that by 1995 at the outside, all the leading hotel chains would have such direct links.

Another area where there is great potential for the application of direct computer access methods is in the central reservations systems operated by the hotel chains themselves. These are capable of processing bookings for an entire hotel chain or group from a single office, linked up to the various individual properties. Using such a system, Forte Travelodge, for example, takes 12,000 to 14,000 reservations a week.

Expansion plans

Some hotel groups, looking forward to the effects of airline deregulation, have identified the potential for business hotels with purpose-built meetings facilities outside London, particularly in the North and Midlands. Improved airlinks from the continent to UK regional airports will make the area around Birmingham, Manchester and Newcastle, as well as Scotland, as accessible as London, but without the capital's high prices and traffic. For example, Jarvis Hotels has launched Summit Conference Centres and plans to widen their availability by purchasing several UK regional hotels; and Whitbread, having acquired hotels in the Leeds/Bradford area, Coventry, Worksop and Ipswich, is planning further expansion at regional sites in the UK.

Questions   1 What special services do business guests require from the hotels they use?

2 Why have airport hotels prospered at a time when city-centre hotels have faced many problems?

3 How can hotels adapt their facilities in order to respond more accurately to the requirements of female business guests?

. . . .

Assignments   1 Role play – in pairs: One person plays the role of the Personnel Manager in a large business: your company has a substantial number of employees 'on the road' all year round. Your employees currently choose their own hotel accommodation when they travel on company business, but you would like to nominate one national/international hotel chain which all your employees would then be obliged to use. In this negotiation, you are interested in obtaining the most substantial reduction possible on the chain's 'rack rate'. Your argument is based on the quantity of business which your company can guarantee the chain.

The other person plays the role of the hotel chain's Director of Sales: your objective in this negotiation is to secure the company's business, but with as high a rate as possible for your chain. Your argument is based on the broad national/international spread of your hotels and the facilities they offer.

2 You are the training manager of one of the hotels used in the *ELLE* magazine survey on pages 165–9. Having read the results of the survey, draw up a training programme for all hotel staff, to be used on a one-day in-service course entitled 'Better Service for Business Guests'.

Key terms   Before moving on to the next chapter, make sure you understand the meaning of the following terms:

Corporate rate

Loyalty clubs

Central reservations systems

Hotel business centres

Guest histories

7

Business travel distribution

INTRODUCTION

Individual business travel concerns the corporate sector – individual employees travelling to do business on behalf of their companies. Few of these employees have either the time or the knowledge required to identify the best travel option, make the necessary travel and accommodation reservations, collect their tickets, and take care of other details such as insurance, visas, and foreign currency. This chapter examines how the retail travel trade serves the corporate sector by providing the link between the various sectors of the business tourism industry and the consumer, the individual business traveller.

WHO TRAVELS ON BUSINESS?

In 1992, approximately £18 billion was spent by UK companies and organisations on their employees' business travel and related expenses. For many companies, travel represents the second largest expense after the salary bill. So, who exactly are the consumers of individual business travel?

The *Business Travel and Expense Management Report 1992* published by American Express Europe Ltd gives an interesting profile of the big spenders in the business travel field.

The report shows that the chances of any particular person being a regular business traveller depend on several factors, namely:

- the kind of business they work for
- their job grade
- their sex.

Industry sector

There is enormous variance in the annual amount spent on business

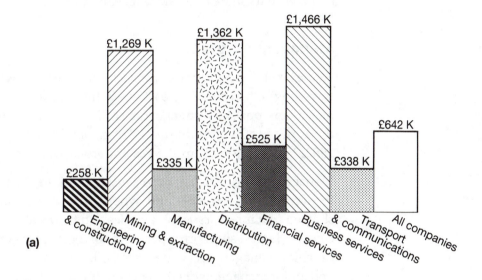

(a)

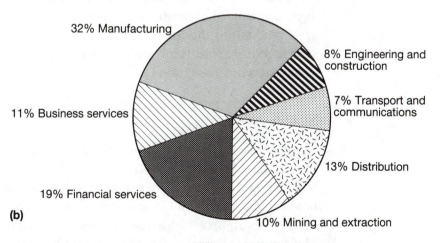

(b)

Figure 7.1(a)   Average travel and expenses (T&E) expenditure per company
Figure 7.1(b)   Share of the total travel and expenses expenditure by industry group
Source: *Business Travel & Expense Management Report 1992*, published by American Express Europe Ltd

travel by individual UK companies, ranging from £3,000 to £5 million. Moreover, a relatively small number of companies are very large spenders on business travel: just 10 per cent of companies account for two-thirds of the total spending. By sector, Business Services, Distribution, and Mining and Extraction (including Oil and Gas) have the highest average expenditure on business travel and expenses per company, amounting to over £1 million per company in each case. Each industry sector's average spending is given in Figures 7.1(a) and (b), along with its share of total travel expenditure.

Management grade

At the level of individual employees, who are those who do most of the travelling? On average, at least one in five employees in British companies incurs business travel expenses in some form, and, according to the American Express *Business Travel and Expense Management Report 1992*, 2 per cent of all employees undertake overseas business travel.

Management grade is an important determining factor when it comes to deciding who travels and where. The American Express report showed that for *domestic* travel, sales and field staff represent, at 27 per cent, the largest single group in terms of their numbers, well in advance of senior management (14 per cent), middle management (19 per cent), and junior management (13 per cent). But the situation is very different with regard to *overseas* travel, where, as may be expected, senior managers account for a significant proportion of the travelling population, at 47 per cent of the total. Middle and junior management and sales staff together account for some 39 per cent of employees who engage in overseas business travel.

Sex

The vast majority of regular business travellers are men. However, the percentage of business travellers who are female is growing steadily, and, it would seem, at an increasing pace. The American Express report noted an increase from 11 per cent to 17 per cent between 1990 and 1992 in the proportion of the total business travellers represented by women. The companies surveyed for the report were asked which proportion of their employees travelling regularly on business were female, and the results, by industry sector, are given in Figure 7.2.

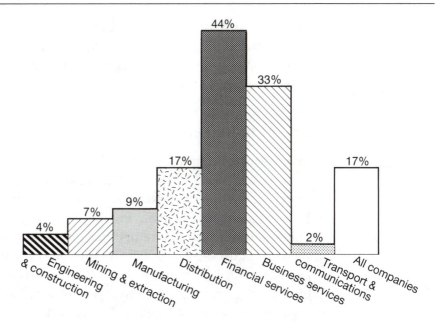

Figure 7.2 Ratio of women travellers to travel and expenses (T&E) incurred in each industry group
Source: *Business Travel & Expense Management Report 1992*, published by American Express Europe Ltd

Clearly, women working in management positions in Financial and Business Service companies have the greatest probability of travelling for work-related purposes.

BUYING BUSINESS TRAVEL

How do companies book the airline and train tickets, hotel accommodation, and hired cars they need in order to get their travelling executives from A to B?

The American Express *Business Travel and Expense Management Report 1992* shows that in the great majority of cases, it is the secretary who picks up the phone to make the necessary travel arrangements for the employees who travel on behalf of the company. Of the companies involved in the survey, 64 per cent said that the travel arrangements for business trips were most frequently made by secretaries and personal assistants.

But, particularly in larger companies with dozens or even hundreds of members of staff regularly travelling on business, there arises the need for someone at managerial level to actually negotiate and manage travel arrangements for employees and to determine the framework within which business travel is purchased by their company. This is often the role of the travel manager.

Travel managers

Many companies employ a specialist travel manager or corporate travel buyer as a central purchaser of travel and as a way of controlling their travel costs. The logic is that one person who centrally purchases travel for a company has more buying muscle to negotiate better prices with hotels and transport operators than all the company's executives – or their secretaries – would have if they each organised their own travel arrangements individually. As well as the advantage gained through bulk buying, having one employee responsible for paying for all a company's travel also means streamlined administrative procedures which save time and help improve efficiency.

Generally, the more employees a company has travelling on its behalf, the more likely it is to employ a travel manager. According to the American Express survey, 56 per cent of companies with 50 or more regular business travellers have a travel manager; 43 per cent of *all* companies employ a travel manager, a significant increase over the 1987 figure of only 28 per cent. Clearly, the realisation of the importance of keeping firm control over their travel expenditure has prompted more and more companies to appoint internal travel managers, who can greatly contribute towards this.

The Institute of Travel Management

Formed in 1956, the Institute of Travel Management (ITM) is the professional association for those who plan and book business travel services on behalf of the staff working within their own companies or organisations. To do this efficiently and economically calls not only for good management and negotiating skills; it also requires an intimate awareness of the current purchasing procedures and availabilities in the inter-related fields of airline, rail and ferry transport, hotel accommodation and car hire. Thus, the central aim of the ITM is to foster ongoing productive communications between the buyers and the suppliers of business travel, to the benefit of both parties. How is this achieved?

Since the travel and accommodation industry is in a constant state of change and development, the need for corporate travel buyers to remain fully up-to-date is paramount. For their part, suppliers to this market – hotel chains, airlines, car hire companies – need a 'window' through which to promote their products and services directly to travel managers. The ITM therefore works to bring the buyers and the suppliers of business travel services together in a mutually beneficial forum. It provides an effective two-way information exchange through an ongoing programme of:

- regular branch meetings

- training and educational events

- social gatherings to foster a 'club' spirit and create new contacts

- regular newsletters – national and regional

- an annual conference.

The ITM annual conference is held in the Spring at a different location each year. The programme provides a valuable insight into the latest travel industry developments, with a comprehensive programme of industry speakers presenting papers on topical issues, discussion forums, and some social networking. A feature of the conference is the industry workshop, where the travel buyers and suppliers have the opportunity to exchange information on requirements and services.

Since 1956, the ITM has become a national authority with a respected voice. It acts as an influential watchdog and spokesman for the business traveller and is regularly consulted by Government departments, the travel trade, and industrial and commercial companies on all aspects of business travel. Also, acting as a consumer body, the ITM participates in many consultative committees, meeting regularly with major airlines and hotel groups.

The International Business Travel Association

An ITM initiative in the late 1960s led to the creation of similarly targeted organisations in a number of overseas countries. Today, under the International Business Travel Association (IBTA) banner, ITM members enjoy the cross-fertilisation benefits of affiliation with other associations of travel managers in Austria, Belgium, Denmark, Finland,

France, Germany, Luxembourg, the Netherlands, Norway, Sweden, Switzerland and the USA.

Implants

Often, the task of organising all of a company's travel needs involves so much administration and clerical work that the travel manager uses a team of assistants who undertake the routine booking and issuing of tickets and other travel documents.

One option open to companies with extensive business travel requirements is to invite a travel agency to set up a branch on their own premises, staffed by travel agency staff who are subcontracted to the company. This is known as a travel agency implant. Those working in the implant remain the employees of the travel agency from which they are subcontracted, but they work on the premises of the company whose travel they organise. One advantage of this arrangement is that the staff of the implant work exclusively for the host company and therefore have the opportunity to develop a personal, deeper understanding of that company's travel needs. They are on the spot to explain itineraries and, if need be, reassure those actually doing the travelling, and they also have the possibility of receiving direct feedback from the company's travelling staff.

According to the American Express survey, 7 per cent of companies have a travel agent working in-house. The presence of an implant automatically releases the travel manager from day-to-day administration, leaving him or her free to undertake a more long-term, strategic role.

CASE
STUDY

Gray Dawes and Lloyds International

Advantages of an implant

COMPANIES ARE at last paying as much attention to their travel budgets as they have traditionally lavished on their advertising expenditures or their vehicle fleets.

Lloyds Bank spends around £5m a year on travel, with just over £2m going on air tickets and almost £3m on hotel accommodation. Last year, just as companies ask for speculative pitches from advertising agencies, so Lloyds asked for proposals from 10 specialist companies on how best to run its travel purchasing. The winner would set up an implant, a four-strong travel agency, plus a messenger, inside Lloyds Hay's Lane building to handle the travel needs of the entire Lloyds group.

After viewing four presentations, Mr Glyn Farrell, who manages Lloyds Personnel and Travel Services, chose Gray Dawes Travel.

It was hardly surprising. The City-based Gray Dawes had first started to work for Lloyds International on an ad hoc basis 10 years ago. Five years ago it established its own team inside Lloyds.

After inspecting the field Mr Farrell stuck with the travel specialists he knew. In three years' time he will keep Gray Dawes on its toes by repeating the trawl.

Mr Farrell reckons that by using a specialist implant travel bureau Lloyds both saves money and operates more efficiently. Apart from local trips of up to about 40 miles, all the travel needs of Lloyds managers go through the Gray Dawes team, which issues tickets, makes hotel bookings, arranges currency, renews passports and obtains visas from an office alongside that of Mr Farrell. Soon there might be satellite offices which might also be capable of issuing tickets, etc.

In his latest review Mr Farrell examined the cost of reviving an internal department, or of putting travel needs out to an outside agency (where there is the danger of being just one client among many) and concluded, as more and more large companies do, that the implant system is the most efficient.

As well as the expertise of the travel team seconded to it, Lloyds saves on the personnel costs, such as pensions and financial perks, of employing its own staff. And if for any reason a face does not fit, Gray Dawes can switch the employee to another client.

Mr Farrell might well see some of the airline or hotel representatives who visit him with tempting discount offers and pass on their suggestions to Gray Dawes, but they handle all the arrangements. Each month he is provided with a detailed computerised breakdown of Lloyds travelling expenses, which enables him to pinpoint which executive went where and at what cost. Over the years the travelling has increased but the budget has stayed roughly the same.

Obviously, the recession has hit the airlines and the hotels hard and they have responded by chasing business customers with attractive offers. But not that attractive. Lloyds and Gray Dawes work with a limited number of airlines in order to secure discounts from achieving target expenditures but, on air travel, discounts rarely top 5 per cent of the listed price, although competition is forcing them marginally higher.

However, Gray Dawes attempts to exploit all the Apex savings available from early booking. Currently British Airways, United, and Virgin (its new mid class is deemed attractive to executives) serve Lloyds' transatlantic requirements. For Europe the need for speed and the general absence of discounts mean that the most efficient flight is booked irrespective of the carrier. The opening up of the skies over Europe could greatly reduce business travel costs on the Continent. Like most companies, Lloyds is cutting back on first-class and business class travel. It not only saves money but conveys an appropriate cost trimming image for the times. Only 150 Lloyds executives are frequent international travellers and around 30 can expect to go first-class.

In the last five years the company has reduced first-class travel by around 20 per cent. Expenditure on business class travelling has also been curbed, although if an airline makes a special promotional offer of upgrades for frequent business fliers (and the new American airlines crossing the Atlantic are particularly inclined to do so) Lloyds is happy to take advantage of the deals. It allows its executive to discover his or her good fortune on arrival at the airport. It does not want to encourage an upgrade mentality in the company.

In the current business climate discounts of up to 50 per cent on hotel accommodation can be secured by Gray Dawes, and not only by dealing with the big international hotel chains. However, if executives complain about a hotel, it is quickly dropped from the schedule. Mr Farrell believes that many companies keep a close watch on their travel costs but waste money on the more expensive area of accommodation.

It is not the travel department's task to fix the budgets: the various departments in Lloyds know their travel needs best. But Mr Farrell helps to police them and to ensure that they stay within the fixed limits and take advantage of any special offers that come on to the market. By having a travel company working exclusively in-house on its behalf, Mr Farrell believes that expertise, efficiency and effort are as good as doubled.

Antony Thorncroft

Source: *The Financial Times*, 25 September 1992.

Business travel agents

In recent years, there has been a marked trend towards companies contracting the entire travel purchasing function out to travel agents. In 1992, 80 per cent of British companies had an appointed travel agent, working with, and in some cases replacing, the travel manager.

From the travelling executive's point of view, there is no extra work involved in using the services of an external travel agent. When planning business trips, they usually contact the travel agent by telephone to pass on their requirements, and the agent makes the necessary bookings, sending the tickets and travellers cheques to the executive's company by courier. Increasingly, also, satellite ticket printers allow airline tickets to be printed and issued remotely, negating the need for courier deliveries or for implants to print them.

The American Express *Business Travel and Expense Management Report 1992* listed the following key advantages to be gained by companies appointing travel agents to handle their business travel:

- Ability to implement a company-wide travel policy (see page 193) which the agency is required to comply with across all your branches and divisions.

- You can ensure that any changes in your travel policy are implemented immediately by the agency.

- Travel suppliers can be compared and selected – by the agency – so that you benefit from corporate and negotiated rates.

- By consolidating your travel purchasing through one agency, you can expect to gain leverage and receive the highest calibre of service.

- Regular management information reports from your travel agent will show travel patterns for all your business travel and related expense incurring employees.

However, for companies, there are many additional advantages in using out-of-house specialist *business* travel agents, or *travel management companies*, as they sometimes like to be called, to organise their travel needs. Those who simply use their local travel agents (who mainly handle holiday bookings in most cases) can miss out on some valuable savings, for example. Specialists who buy a lot of travel often have access to some of the best discounts and special offers available.

A good business travel agent will be able to secure the best deals for the client company, negotiating a path through the maze of special prices, discounts and incentives on offer.

There is no doubt that business travel agents represent the most demanding and dynamic sector of the retail travel trade. The work is high-pressure, but the rewards earned through dealing with corporate clients can be extremely high.

Satisfying the growing demands of multinational company clients for *global* travel networks is the latest challenge facing the business travel retail sector. David Whittaker, the chairman of the Guild of Business Travel Agents, described these new challenges in an interview with David Churchill of the *Financial Times* in September 1992: 'Major multinational companies increasingly demand from their travel agents a global network so that they can arrange, monitor, and control their travel costs worldwide.' The MORI report for Wagon-lits confirms this: four out of five decision makers interviewed for the survey put a travel agent's ability to cope with the worldwide needs of their companies as an important consideration for the future. In order to respond to these demands, the leading travel groups, such as the world's top five – American Express, Carlson, Wagon-lits, Thomas Cook and the Japan Travel Bureau – have made strenuous efforts to establish international networks, through acquisition, in recent years.

The advent of *computer reservations systems* (CRSs) has enabled traditional business travel agents to expand into providing full travel management services, increasingly on a global scale. Before looking more closely at the relationship between business travel agents and their client companies, it is important to investigate the impact which CRSs have had and are continuing to have on the world of business travel.

Computer reservations systems

Speed, efficiency and accuracy are the qualities sought after by those buying and selling business travel, and information and telecommunications technology is the powerful tool used to achieve these goals.

The use of computer reservations systems (CRSs) to make travel reservations has been a feature of the international travel industry for many years. Such systems originated in the USA, where they were developed and dominated by the airlines. Their original purpose was simply to provide an automated means of storing and managing data about the airlines' flights, availability and fares. In those days, they were little more than electronic airline timetables.

An important step forward came when the computer terminals – the access points to the central database – were available at the point of sale: in other words, in the travel agencies themselves. Travel agents could then use their terminals to search the airline's database, obtain price and availability information, and make the actual reservation. This was more efficient than the previous system of a travel agent telephoning the airline's reservation office and speaking to a clerk who would be using an identical terminal.

The next advance came when the CRSs moved away from simply selling the products of the single airline which owned them towards becoming systems which held not only other airlines' products, but also other travel-related products such as hotel rooms and car rental. This process was made possible by the creating of direct on-line links with hotel groups' and car rental companies' own existing computerised reservations systems. These facilities normally served the central reservation offices of these companies and were usually known as CRO systems. Discussing the importance of CROs in an article in the February 1993 edition of *Tourism Management*, Gilbert Archdale, a consultant specialising in the travel and tourism marketing applications of information technology, wrote,

> The prime market for the majority of (companies with CROs) is the businessman or woman. Business travel is normally considered a market where product price is not always ranked as high in determining customer choice as the anticipated standard of the product and the certainty of its delivery. Thus, an effective CRO can deliver branded products to a known customer base with little fear of a breakdown in the communications process.

An example of a 'branded product' would be a room in a Hilton hotel, or the rental of a Hertz car for a few days.

It is the combination of CROs and CRSs which enables the travel agent to book a range of travel and travel-related products directly, without the need to telephone any intermediary. Now, using a desktop personal computer plugged into a telephone socket, it is possible to arrange a complex itinerary, check late seat availability on different airlines, print out tickets, make hotel reservations and hire cars. As the process of integrating airlines' CRSs with other providers' CROs advances, travel agents will be able to provide an even more efficient and comprehensive service to their business clients. Although airlines still dominate CRSs, hotels, car rental companies, the ferries and railways are increasingly seeing the advantages of CRSs as a powerful means of distribution.

CRSs can also be used to provide an improved tailored service to travellers and their companies. Travel agents can use their technology to build up corporate and customer profiles by storing them in the CRS. In this way, the travel agent has available at the touch of a button information such as a particular company's policy on flight class or preferred airline for its employees, or for example whether a traveller is a smoker or requires special meals.

By the early 1990s, there were about ten major CRSs operating in different parts of the world, including the Sabre, Apollo and Worldspan systems for the USA and the still-developing Amadeus and Galileo systems in Europe, both originally set up as counter-measures to the powerful American systems. Ten years previously, the large American CRSs, which had been very successful and very profitable in their own country, had begun expanding outside the US, with varying degrees of success. In Europe, events moved much more slowly. The airlines could not agree on one system and developments split into two camps: Amadeus and Galileo.

The latest development in the rise of CRSs is towards consolidation, the attempt to provide a truly global service for both product vendors and travel agency users, through partnership agreements between CRSs. In this, the CRSs are progressing along the same path as the large travel companies, who are increasingly moving towards providing global travel services for their clients. In September 1992, Amadeus, Worldspan (owned by Delta, Northwest, and TWA) and Abacus (owned by five Asian airlines) announced a cooperation agreement by which they would interconnect their respective CRSs. Similarly, in January 1993, Galileo, Apollo, and Gemini, the Canadian CRS, signed a combination agreement to create Galileo International, the first truly global CRS. Galileo International will be owned 50 per cent by European airlines – Aer Lingus, Alitalia, Austrian Airlines, British Airways, KLM Royal Dutch Airlines, Olympic Airways, Swissair, and TAP Air Portugal – and 50 per cent owned by North American airlines – Air

Canada, United Airlines, and USAir. The new company will serve 25,000 travel agency locations worldwide.

It is clear that very soon CRSs will be the main point and method of sale for all business travel products in travel agencies. With more and more multinational companies operating worldwide, CRSs are also becoming vital tools for travel agents coping with their demands for a global travel network. And, as the speed with which business is done increases and customers increasingly make last-minute travel decisions, there is intense pressure on business travel agents to process and deliver travel documents rapidly. All of this means that it is now virtually impossible for any travel agent in the business sector to function without the use of a CRS.

WAGON-LITS BUSINESS TRAVEL SURVEY

In November 1992, Market & Opinion Research International (MORI) was commissioned by Wagon-lits Travel to undertake a survey investigating the relationship between companies and the business travel agents they used. Several aspects of the way in which companies view the travel agents with which they do business were examined, and the results are set out below.

The process of selecting a business travel agent

First of all, *how often do companies review their existing business travel relationships?* While around one in five of the decision makers claimed to review their existing arrangements every two or three years, over a third said they did so on an annual basis. This was found to be the most popular reviewing period. Evaluating an agency more frequently than this was found to be rare: only one in ten decision makers does this more than once a year.

Secondly, *who has a say in which business travel agent is selected?* The decision about which business travel agent to use was found to be generally a shared one in any company. Almost half the decision makers claimed to canvass travellers' views when choosing an agency; but, equally, half did not do so. But much more likely to be taken on board, it would seem, are the views of the *bookers* within an organisation: 61 per cent of decision makers said that they took into account the opinions of the bookers. One secretary was quoted as saying:

> Good agencies are like good hairdressers – you like to stick with them.

With such a high rate of secretarial involvement in the selection process, Richard Lovell, the managing director of Wagon-lits Travel, made the following comment: 'It is clear where we must place our emphasis. The role of the secretary is highly influential and we must meet that challenge.'

Those travelling on business might do well, too, to remember the power which their secretaries have over their travel arrangements. For example, secretaries' influence can often have an impact on the class of travel or the category of hotel chosen – something which their bosses ought to bear in mind when browsing in the airport gift shop. The MORI survey identified a high proportion of disgruntled secretaries, three-quarters of whom 'never' or 'rarely' received a gift brought back from their bosses' business trips!

Next, *which are the factors most sought-after when decision makers are looking to appoint an agency*? In the current economic climate, it is hardly surprising that competitive pricing tops the list – put first by 59 per cent of decision makers. A rather more subjective measure, 'professionalism', is sought after by 47 per cent. The range of services offered by the agency was mentioned by a third. The survey notes, however, that many respondents remarked that competitive pricing is not sufficient on its own, but that there was also a strong need to be able to trust an agency. One decision maker was quoted as saying:

> . . . using a travel agent is no different from using any other service. You are buying a service as opposed to a product . . . you want that product delivered to your door in the best way and most economical way you can get it.

Travel expertise (17 per cent) and knowledge of a customer's business (6 per cent) were other factors considered important.

Services used

The booking of flights was found to be the prime service for which almost all of the companies involved in the survey used business travel agents. Rail travel and hotels follow, with around three-quarters of bookers and decision makers using these services. Car hire, despite being less widely used, was found to be still considered a main service by well over half the respondents. Just under half of them used their business travel agencies for obtaining passports and visas, and around a third used their agencies to provide foreign exchange, travellers' cheques and travel insurance.

Service – satisfaction and importance

Clients' level of satisfaction with the overall service received from their business travel agents was found to be exceptionally high: 96 per cent of bookers and 95 per cent of decision makers were satisfied with the general service offered. The factors considered to be the most important to overall service from a business travel agent were as follows. *Accuracy* came first, followed by *speed of response*. Third on the list was the need to have *confidence* in your contact, reinforcing earlier comments about the importance of being able to place absolute trust in an agency. *Level of knowledge* was also found to contribute a large part to overall service standards. The other factors found to play an important role in the quality of overall service were: a responsive attitude, accessibility of contact, relationships with the contact, and the ability to secure good route deals for clients.

THE GUILD OF BRITISH TRAVEL AGENTS

In 1967, six London business travel agents who felt that their needs were not fully represented by the Association of British Travel Agents formed the Guild of British Travel Agents (GBTA) to maintain a continuing dialogue between the increasing number of travel agents whose principal activity was business at corporate level. Until that date, no other organisation existed to promote the specific interests of business travel agents and their clients.

In the ensuing years, the GBTA developed into one of the world's most exclusive and influential travel trade organisations, dedicated to safeguarding and developing the interests of the business traveller. Its membership now comprises 41 of the UK's leading travel agents, which in themselves have over 1,900 branch offices and approximately 17,350 staff. Members include the giant multiples, American Express, Thomas Cook, Hogg Robinson, Wagon-lits, Carlson, and Pickfords, as well as the UK's leading independent business travel specialists. GBTA members now handle 75–80 per cent of the agency-generated business air traffic in Britain, and its members' turnover totalled almost £3½ billion in 1992. Membership is strictly by invitation only, with each new member undergoing a rigorous vetting procedure before being invited to join the ranks. All hold International Air Transport Association (IATA) licences and must have been members of ABTA for at least 5 years.

The GBTA uses a variety of methods to raise standards and improve the quality of travel for its clients. Prime among these is an ongoing dialogue at the highest level with such influential organisations as the European Commission, British Airports Authority plc, the Civil Aviation Authority, airlines and hotel groups. In addition, the GBTA engages in government lobbying at the highest level. It has its own parliamentary consultant, Sir Anthony Grant, who, on the one hand, keeps the GBTA informed of relevant developments on the parliamentary scene and, on the other, represents business travel agents' views to those who matter in and around Whitehall. This arrangement has given the Guild a voice in key issues such as new airport terminals and runways, improved road and rail links to prime hubs, and a wide array of other matters of concern to the business traveller.

The following example of successful GBTA lobbying is given by the Guild's Chief Executive, David Reynolds:

> In the late 1980s, the European flag carriers (except British Airways) were taking a very restrictive attitude towards emerging low cost carriers such as British Midland and Air Europe. The flag carriers were refusing to accept the new entrants' documents, which meant that passengers travelling, for example, out to Frankfurt on Air Europe and who wished to change their return to Lufthansa were being asked to pay for a new ticket.
>
> We felt that this was not in the interests of the business travellers, the Agents who serve them, nor, in the long term, of the carrier involved.
>
> We therefore wrote to each of the carriers, Air France, Alitalia, Lufthansa, SAS and Aer Lingus, some of whose replies were quite

arrogant and which in summation said 'we will choose with whom we do business'. Accordingly, we went to the European Commission, who have the power to fine a carrier up to 10 per cent of their turnover. They put pressure on these carriers who eventually caved in, thus providing the passenger with a better service and less hassle.

The exception was Aer Lingus, who were very concerned at having to face competition from British Midland on their flagship Dublin–London route. Again we put pressure on Aer Lingus. I saw the Chief Executive personally, but they refused to budge. Again we went to the European Commission but they were unable to change the Irish stance. Eventually, a case was filed by the Commission against Aer Lingus, and a hearing was held. At the hearing, Aer Lingus claimed that there had been no complaints from travel agents. The Commission immediately asked for copies of our correspondence with Aer Lingus, and these were faxed to them. These completely demolished Aer Lingus' case, and they were fined over £½ million. Needless to say, Aer Lingus now have an interline agreement with British Midland.

Apart from keeping up the pressure of lobbying in key areas, the GBTA has also embarked upon a campaign to create even greater professionalism and quality in the industry. It initiated, in collaboration with ABTA's National Training Board and City & Guilds, the first ever qualifications specifically geared to the business travel industry. Now, over 700 staff hold these Business Travel Certificates. Initially designed for Guild members, these courses are now available to the business travel world at large, a move towards raising standards generally in the industry. In 1993, a Master of Business Administration (MBA) programme was launched in conjunction with the University of Brighton.

The final sphere of activity of the GBTA is that of technology, which they regard as essential to the development of international travel and to the infrastructure required to support the business traveller. To this end, the GBTA employs its own consultant to ensure that its members are at the forefront of technological progress and that new airline computer reservations systems meet the needs of members and their clients. Through its consultant, the GBTA aims to build a close relationship between the CRS companies and its own members. The main benefit to GBTA members of this policy is that they receive early sight of the latest developments in technology, while the CRS companies can ensure that their technology is thoroughly tested in a live situation.

THE GUILD OF EUROPEAN BUSINESS TRAVEL AGENTS

Following the success of the British Guild, initial discussions were held in 1989 with groups of business travel agents in other EU countries, with a view to forming a European Guild. It was felt that since the airlines were forming bigger and bigger marketing alliances to become mega airlines, and the computer reservations systems were doing likewise, it was important for Europe's business travel world to make itself heard collectively.

The Guild of European Business Travel Agents (GEBTA) now has eight national guilds representing over 200 members in Belgium, Denmark, France, Ireland, Italy, the Netherlands, Spain and the UK, which speak with a unified voice on pan-European issues such as VAT on air fares, air traffic control, and airline competition. It has full-time representation in Brussels for liaison with and for lobbying the EU. An example of GEBTA's effective lobbying in that quarter was seen in 1992 when, after two years' work, it was instrumental in postponing the proposed imposition of VAT on international air fares, an issue which will now be reconsidered in 1996. This was achieved by constant lobbying of officials in Brussels and by harnessing GEBTA's national Guilds to lobby their individual MEPs.

With the $10 billion turnover of its members, GEBTA is already a force to be reckoned with, and is set to expand even further. The participation of Germany, Greece and Portugal is now being sought, and leading EFTA countries such as Switzerland, Sweden and Norway are also being lined up.

FORMAL TRAVEL POLICY

A way of controlling travel costs

With travel representing a major item of corporate expenditure, many companies have introduced formal travel policies for their employees, as a way of controlling business travel expenditure. The *Business Travel and Expense Management Report 1992* published by American Express found that out of the companies surveyed (all of which had a minimum of 10 staff incurring travelling expenses):

- 52% had a formal, written, travel policy

- 43% had informal guidelines only, and

- 5% had no travel policy at all.

Generally, it was found that companies with larger numbers of employees travelling regularly on business were more likely to have a formal travel policy. Of companies with fewer than 20 staff travelling on business, 29 per cent were found to have a written policy, while this proportion rose to 71 per cent among companies with 50 or more regular business travellers. No great variation was found from sector to sector in the percentage of companies having a formal travel policy. According to the survey, Financial Services companies were most likely to have such a policy (64 per cent) and Distribution companies least likely (42 per cent).

Formulation of a company's travel policy is generally done at Board or Management Committee level, although in some cases, this can be a function of Administration or the Personnel department. Enforcement of the policy, however, is usually delegated to department managers, Accounts or Administration.

The American Express report gives the following five recommendations to companies planning to introduce a formal travel policy for the first time:

1 Decide who should be responsible for drawing up the policy and what should be included in it.

2 Agree on a reasonable balance between traveller comfort and cost-effectiveness.

3 Ensure that the document defines the company's overall travel policy and philosophy and spells out all the guidelines clearly.

4 Distribute the policy to everyone involved with incurring or managing travel and related expenditure, including your travel suppliers.

5 Establish clear procedures for enforcing, maintaining and reviewing the policy.

What does a company's formal travel policy include?

Travel policies are most commonly used by companies to exercise some degree of control over their employees' transport and accommodation arrangements for business travel.

The class of travel allowed, for example, on air travel or on train journeys is usually a feature of the travel policy, since these are such important items in any company's travel budget. Whether executives travel first, business, or economy class by air, or first or standard class by train, is most often determined by the business traveller's management grade, but can also be affected by the length of the journey or the time of day or night the journey takes place. The MORI survey for Wagon-lits identified some companies where, as an economy measure, the travel policy had been amended so that only employees with bad backs could still travel first class by air (needless to say, the number of employees suddenly afflicted by bad backs was staggeringly high!).

The American Express survey found that most companies (76 per cent) exercised some form of control over employees' air travel, while 47 per cent of the companies surveyed had written rules or guidelines relating to their employees' use of hotel accommodation, with some (39 per

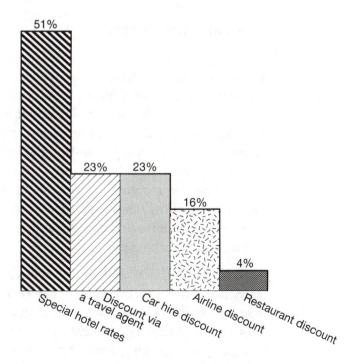

Figure 7.3 The types of deal companies have with suppliers
Source: *Business Travel & Expense Management Report 1992*, published by American Express Europe Ltd

cent) actually stipulating that certain hotels should be used (usually those with which they have negotiated special rates).

Special discounts and corporate rates are widespread, especially for companies with a large volume of business travel. Of the companies surveyed for the American Express report, 56 per cent were found to have some form of discount or corporate rate in at least one of the three main spending categories: air travel, accommodation and car rental. It is another function of the travel policy to communicate to travelling employees (and to those purchasing travel and accommodation on their behalf) any such special arrangements which their company has negotiated with suppliers and to spell out the guidelines for employees' use of these suppliers' services. The American Express report found that negotiated discounts for companies are most commonly to be found with hotels, but Figure 7.3 shows that special deals for companies are by no means restricted to this sector.

TRENDS

Economy measures

Perhaps more than for any other sector of the business tourism industry, the fortunes of business travel tend to follow very closely those of the economy in general. When the economy is buoyant and the level of economic activity is high, it is reasonable to assume that the level of business travel will also be high. Conversely, during a recession, with many companies going into liquidation and a slump in economic activity, business travel will be hit accordingly. (Set against this general rule, some commentators point to the need for *increased* travel in recessionary times, as competition for a shrinking pool of buyers becomes more intense and companies are consequently obliged to seek out and conquer new markets.)

Half of the decision makers interviewed in the 1992 MORI survey carried out on behalf of Wagon-lits Travel said that their companies had tightened their belts by amending travel policy to trade down in class of travel or hotel. Almost two in five bookers believed that their company was making fewer business trips in view of the economic climate, although only 17 per cent saw their businesses making shorter trips as a cost-cutting measure.

In many cases, companies' economy measures as identified by the MORI survey were presented as a move towards a more democratic 'everybody equal' travel policy, whereby all members of staff travelled in the same class of transport and used the same grade of hotel accommodation. But, since it was usually senior management whose class of travel was downgraded to bring it in line with the rest of the staff, the real, cost-cutting intentions behind such changes in company policy were only thinly disguised.

The situation as reported by the American Express *Business Travel and Expense Management Report 1992* showed the same signs of slowdown in companies' spending on travel. The survey showed a marked curb on travel expenditure during 1991, with the engineering and construction sector the worst hit.

FUTURE TRENDS

Light at the end of the tunnel?

Despite the prevailing gloom, the American Express report suggested that this belt-tightening regime was not expected to outride the recession. Most companies interviewed predicted an upward movement in travel and related spending between 1992 and 1994, expecting it to increase in line with company revenue or even to increase faster than revenue. Only 14 per cent of companies expected their spending on business travel to decline relative to total turnover. The general impression given was favourable: that business as a whole regarded travel activity by their employees as an essential condition for growth.

What seems certain is that in the future, corporate management will be faced with the challenge of finding new ways of rationalising business travel, minimising costs and managing the necessary expenditure in the most cost-effective way.

Cost-saving strategies which seem set to become more widespread include:

- The creation and adoption of a formal, written, travel policy. To remain effective, this will be regularly reviewed to allow for changes in the company's own needs as well as changes in the travel industry itself.

- More careful price comparison and discount negotiation with suppliers such as airlines and hotels, which are facing increasing competition.

- The use of specialist business travel agents able to negotiate lower rates on air fares and accommodation on behalf of the company.

However, all cost-saving strategies must be considered in the light of one question: how far should companies go in their cost-cutting measures? It is important that, in their corporate enthusiasm to control costs, those in command should not forget the purpose of business travel: namely, to enable employees to travel in order to do business effectively, on behalf of the company and in the company's interests. The opportunity to rest, and, if necessary, work in comfort should be essential features of business travel. Travel, even at executive level, is tiring and stressful enough, and there is little point in company employees arriving at their destination red-eyed and exhausted after a sleepless night flying over the Atlantic in economy class crammed in between a crying baby and a portable video game enthusiast.

Company accountants and cost-hacking travel managers should also be made aware of 'false economies'. Cheaper airline tickets, for example, often have the disadvantage of being very inflexible. Travellers missing their plane home because a meeting went on longer than expected may find that they have to pay a hefty premium in order to change their return flight. On long-haul flights, such as those to the Far East, cheaper flights can include multiple stop-overs, which can add several hours to the journey, and perhaps the loss of a whole working day back in the office.

Where will travelling executives be heading to in the years ahead? According to the MORI survey, France was the European country to which British companies thought their business travel was most likely to expand over the next two to three years – perhaps making use of the Channel Tunnel; this was closely followed by Germany. Eastern Europe was also selected as a future business travel growth area by around one in five of the decision makers interviewed. The general indication was that it was more likely to be larger firms (those with over 300 staff) who were anticipating expansion into these countries. Just over a quarter of decision makers did not foresee any European growth at all in business travel within their organisation.

The countries outside Europe expected to become more frequent business travel destinations were the USA and the Far East. But about a third of decision makers believed that over the next few years their companies' business travel to countries outside Europe would not increase at all.

Questions

1 What are the advantages to a company of having an implant for arranging its travel?

2 What impact have computer reservations systems had on business travel retail?

3 What features of the service they receive from their business travel agents do companies consider to be the most important?

Assignments

1 Many travel agents employ specialist staff to handle the travel arrangements of local businesses. Part of their job is to go out and make presentations to local companies in order to persuade them to use the agency to buy their business travel. Prepare and make a 15-minute presentation (using visual aids if possible) in which you make the case for a local manufacturing business using your agency instead of organising its own business travel.

2 Contact a number of large companies and public sector organisations in your area requesting a copy of their travel policy. Compare the responses you receive. (If this is a group assignment, make sure no company or organisation is contacted by more than one person.)

Key terms   Make sure you understand the meaning of the following terms:

Travel manager

Implant

Business travel agencies

Computer reservations systems

Company travel policy

Bibliography

....

Reports

The European Incentive Travel Industry 1990

A survey conducted by Greene Belfield-Smith into the size, volume and contents of incentive travel in Europe. Commissioned by the European Travel Commission.

Touche Ross,
Greene Belfield-Smith Division,
Victoria House,
Vernon Place,
London WC1B 4DB
Tel: 071 936 3000

The Exhibition Industry – The Facts

Designed to assist users of exhibitions in the planning of their marketing programmes, and to give reliable data to all who stage or service exhibitions.

The Exhibition Industry Federation,
254 Upper Richmond Road West,
London SW14 8AG
Tel: 071 582 6869

How Conference Organisers Choose Meetings Venues

An in-depth investigation of how organisers in major companies make venue-purchasing decisions.

Meetings Industry Association,
34 High Street,
Broadway,
Worcestershire WR12 7DT
Tel: 0386 858572

Key Note Report – Business Travel

A review of the UK business travel industry and trends in foreign business travellers visiting the UK.

> **Key Note Publications Ltd,**
> 28/42 Banner Street,
> London EC1Y 8QE
> *Tel: 071 253 3906*

Survey of UK Business Travel and Entertainment Expense Management

A biennial survey of practices in the management of travel and entertainment expenditure by UK companies.

> **American Express Europe Ltd,**
> Travel Management Services,
> Portland House,
> Stag Place,
> London SW1E 5BZ
> *Tel: 071 834 5555*

UK Conference Market Survey 1990

A survey conducted to quantify the size and nature of the conference market.

> **Coopers & Lybrand Deloitte,**
> Hillgate House,
> 26 Old Bailey,
> London EC4M 7PL
> *Tel: 071 583 5000*

English Tourist Board/British Tourist Authority publications

Business Tourism: A Market Profile

An examination of the size, structure and requirements of the business tourism market and a review of current trends.

Insights

Insights is the English Tourist Board's bi-monthly subscription-based marketing intelligence publication. It contains an invaluable blend of essential facts, statistics, marketing commentary and analysis on all aspects of leisure and business tourism.

International Passenger Survey (IPS): Overseas Conference Visitors to the UK 1990 & Overseas Trade Fair/Exhibition Visitors to the UK

The *IPS* is a continuous large-scale survey of visitors entering and leaving the UK which is sponsored and commissioned by the Department of Employment. The information on conferences and trade fairs/exhibitions is obtained from special analyses of standard IPS data commissioned by the BTA.

These publications are available from the ETB/BTA, Department D, 24 Grosvenor Gardens, London SW1W 0ET. *Tel: 081 846 9000.*

Magazines

Business Traveller

Tower Publishing Services,
Tower House,
Sovereign Park,
Market Harborough,
Leicestershire LE16 9EF
Tel: 0858 468888

Conference & Exhibition Fact Finder

Batiste Publications Ltd
Pembroke House,
Campsbourne Road,
Hornsey,
London N8 7PE
Tel: 081 340 3291

Conference & Incentive Travel

Tower Publishing Services,
Tower House,
Sovereign Park,
Market Harborough,
Leicestershire LE16 9EF
Tel: 0858 468888

Executive Travel

Reed Travel Group,
Francis House,
11 Francis Street,
London SW1P 1BZ
Tel: 071 828 8989

Exhibition Bulletin

The London Bureau,
266–272 Kirkdale,
Sydenham,
London SE26 4RZ
Tel: 081 778 2288

Incentive Travel

Incentive Travel,
4 New Bridge Street,
Fleet Street,
London EC4V 6AA
Tel: 071 583 0077

Meetings & Incentive Travel

Conference and Travel Publications Ltd,
Media House,
The Square,
Forest Row,
RH18 5EP
Tel: 0342 824044

Index

....

Books available in our ABTA NTB series

Pitman Publishing has combined its professional expertise as the leading vocational publisher with the Association of British Travel Agents' National Training Board (ABTA NTB), the lead body responsible for setting the training standards within the travel and tourism industry. Together we will ensure that we are at the forefront with learning material specifically written for all those who want to know more and who want to advance within this very competitive field of work.

'The Association of British Travel Agents National Training Board (ABTA NTB) is committed to the training of personnel within the travel and tourism industry. The most effective way to ensure that staff within the industry are professionally qualified is for them to have an NVQ. The application of the government's Education and Training Development scheme to the travel and tourism industry means that at least 53,000 within the field will have taken an NVQ or unit of an NVQ by 1996.'

Peter Aley, Director of Strategic Plans and Co-ordination, ABTA National Training Board.

Our titles prepared in consultation with ABTA NTB are recommended as **essential** reading for trainees taking NVQs/SVQs at all levels and other travel industry qualifications to degree level. They will provide all users with important underpinning knowledge in their chosen area of specialisation. **This knowledge is crucial if trainees are to understand the systems involved in the travel and tourism industry and how best to utilise their potential in the work area.**

The books cater for all levels of experience and cover a wide variety of subjects in the travel and tourism industry. They will prove invaluable to trainees and experienced practitioners alike. To survive and prosper everyone within the industry must keep up to date with the changing laws, policies and trends which affect travel and tourism - these books will help you on your way.

How to order:

All books can be ordered through your regular bookshop or supplier.

In case of difficulty, send your remittance in full, to

Southport Book Distributors,
12/14 Slaidburn Crescent, Southport, Merseyside, PR9 9YF.
Tel: 0704 26881, Fax: 0704 231970.

If you would like further information about the full range of our travel and tourism titles, please contact the Marketing Department at our London office at

Pitman Publishing,
128 Long Acre, London WC2E 9AN.
Tel: 071-379 7383, Fax: 071-240 5771.

The Business of Tourism

4th edition

CHRISTOPHER HOLLOWAY
Professor of Tourism Management, Bristol Business School, University of the West of England.

The Business of Tourism provides a basic understanding of the nature, structure and organisation of the tourist industry.

The book examines the role of tourism in the economic development of a country and explores the relationship between public and private sector tourism. The operations of each part of the industry – tourist attractions, carriers, accommodation, tour operation, retailing, tourist offices and ancillary services – are described in detail. Often overlooked aspects of the industry receive attention, such as the role of tourist guides and the importance of insurance, foreign exchange and credit.

Key features
- published in association with ABTA National Training Board
- well-established bestseller
- each chapter has clear objectives, self-assessment questions and assignments
- numerous photographs, maps and diagrams included

What's new about the fourth edition
- thoroughly up-to-date throughout
- includes a new section on hospitality
- also covers travel retailing and support services
- addresses the issues of the social and environmental impact of tourism on the receiving country
- contains an up-date on the airline industry to include the latest guidelines from the Civil Aviation Authority (CAA)

Contents
An introduction to tourism / The history of tourism: from its origins to the age of steam / Tourism in the twentieth century / The economics of tourism / Tourist motivation and behaviour / The structure and organisation of the travel and tourism industry / Passenger transport: the aviation business / Water-borne passenger transport / Road and rail passenger transport / The hospitality sector: accommodation and catering services / Visitor attractions and visitor management / Tour operating / Travel retailing / Ancillary tourism services / The structure and role of public sector tourism / Tourism design and management / The social and environmental impact of tourism/ Bibliography / Index

0 273 60130 X

Tourism

2nd edition

ROB DAVIDSON
Visiting Lecturer in Tourism at the Universities of Montpellier, Lille and Lyon, and former Education and Training Manager at the British Tourism Authority.

Tourism is an introductory text which covers the basics of travel and tourism. It provides a very useful background to students taking any tourism qualification below degree level. Textual and photographic amendments have been made as necessary to suit NVQ requirements.

The text is organised into 11 well-structured chapters covering all aspects of travel and tourism including: definitions of tourism; a brief history of tourism; travel and transport, accommodation and catering; leisure, recreation and business facilities; tourism promotion at home and abroad; the geography of tourism; the impact of tourism on the environment, economy, culture and community; and working in the industry.

Each chapter contains stimulating material drawn from a variety of sources, diagrams, statistics and photographs as well as exercises, assignments and role plays to encourage an investigative approach to the subject.

'...an ideal workbook.' **Travel and Tourism Programme News**

Contents

Tourism and tourists / The geography of tourism / Transport / The retail travel trade / Accommodation and catering / Tourist attractions and business facilities / Tourism promotion and tourist information / The impact of tourism on the environment / The impact of tourism on the economy / The impact of tourism on culture and communities / Tourism employment and skills

0 273 60129 6

Other titles include

Tourism in Europe
Rob Davidson, Visiting Lecturer in Tourism, Universities of Montpellier, Lyon and Lille, and former Education and Training Manager at the British Tourism Authority.
0 273 03829 X

Travel Geography
2nd edition
Rosemary Burton, Senior Lecturer, Department of Town and Country Planning, University of West of England, Bristol
0 273 60203 9

The Business of Tour Operations
3rd edition
Pat Yale, Freelance Journalist
0 273 60177 6

Interpersonal Skills for Travel and Tourism
Lisa Burton, Open Learning Development Officer. Formerly with Flexible Training Services.
0 273 60467 8

Information Technology in Travel and Tourism
Gary Inkpen, Director of Inkpen Associates, an independent IT consultancy firm
0 273 60229 2

Marketing for Tourism
2nd edition
J Christopher Holloway, Professor of Tourism Management, Bristol Business School and **Ronald V Plant**, well known consultant to the travel and tourism industry.
0 273 03844 3

Finance for Travel and Tourism
Beulah Cope, Tourism Lecturer, University of Brighton.
0 273 60178 4

Travel Agency Law
John Downes, Senior Lecturer in Law and **Tricia Paton**, Lecturer in Law, Dundee Institute of Technology.
0 273 60227 6

The Implementation of the European Directive on Package Travel
Alan Bowen, Head of Legal Services ABTA and Company Secretary for ABTA
0 273 60389 2